MAKING

AUSTRALIA

FAIR

John White has written an engaging book in a colloquial style. Reflecting on COVID 19 as a 'circuit breaker', he urges us to rethink accepted systems of government, public finance and land ownership.

The reader will be invited to consider alternatives to political and economic systems which White correctly identifies as having failed. He urges spiritual transformation as a path to reform and restoration of human relationships with each other and the Creation.

The ideas are thought provoking and worthy of further investigation.

Right Reverend Kate Wilmot
Assistant Bishop of Perth, WA

Real change is possible even for us humans. John and I have been privileged to see this capacity played out among the most devastated of our fellow citizens – victims and offenders of horrific crimes meeting together to seek out a way forward. John is right – we are capable of making our precious planet habitable again. Will we heed the call? Some will, but how many? It remains to be seen. There is however a larger story of which we are just a part and the unfolding of that story awaits each one of us.

Michael Cockram AM
Barrister and Solicitor (Retired)

This book presents the reader with a collection of ideas and eloquent solutions to the future of being fair, exposing the many myths around current economic theory and the power of the very few over the many. It sets out a good argument for the common good and a redirection of economic policy making.

Dr. Brian Steels
Behaviourist & Criminologist

MAKING
AUSTRALIA
Fair

Challenging
Privilege, Wealth & Power

JOHN G. WHITE

COVENTRY
PRESS

Published in Australia by
Coventry Press
33 Scoresby Road
Bayswater VIC 3153

ISBN 9780648861294

Catalogue-in-Publication entry is available from the National Library of
Australia http://catalogue.nla.gov.au

Cover design by Ian James – www.jgd.com.au
Text design by Coventry Press
Typeset in Tex Gyre Pagella

Printed in Australia

Contents

Acknowledgments

I truly acknowledge the homelands of the traditional people of the land which we all share today. The Ballardong Noongar people who, over 60,000 years of existence, have made this place in which I live a truly remarkable story of survival and coexistence.

Although we share a common ground, it is with great honour that I acknowledge and pay due respect to the Noongar elders both past and present, who have been watching over and caring for this land through ancient times until now.

It is those cultural customs of lore, language and land use that resonate with me and my peers more and more as I 'listen' with an open heart and generous spirit.

As a respected Noongar brother recently said to me, *'Nitcha Noongar Boodja Nyinning, Gnulla Moort, Gnulla Wern, Gnulla Boodja*:

'This is Noongar land on which you are sitting – our people, our spirit, our land.'

My hope is that our acknowledgment is always sincerely meant. Perhaps for some of us it provides a little less discomfort about the great gulf between First and Second Nations peoples. Whatever the case, our acknowledgment is empty unless and until we enact the radical changes that honour our sentiments and words; until, of ourselves, we require and facilitate 'truth telling,' and all subsequent action essential for us to become a single, honouring, integrated nation.

I hope you'll read on as we investigate what is needed for Australia to become 'fair' – not only for our Aboriginal sisters and brothers – as pivotal and desperate as is that need – but fair for every citizen, every creature, and the land itself.

Thank you

To Jennifer, my life companion, friend and supporter. Thank you for our forty-six years together, and for our children, Emma and Benjamin, and grandsons, Hamish, Nathan and Ian.

To my friends and teachers, to every voice of truth and justice to which I have had access, and to mentors past and present who see correctly, think wisely and act compassionately and courageously to transform unjust structures of society, thank you!

To my sisters and brothers of the Whadjuk, Yued and Ballardong Noongar peoples of 'Dudja', the beautiful land location I am privileged to share with you, and to all First Nations Peoples throughout Australia, thank you!

To all who sense something is radically wrong with economic, political and social systems in Australian society, and want to see change that is good for all, continue to speak up and contribute what you are able to.

To my editor, Hugh, publicist, Nicci, and the team at Coventry, thank you for your professional and personal assistance and support.

To you, my reader: thank you for being interested and engaged in the issues contained herein. Let's all 'wake-up' and, together, make this wonderful country 'fair'!

John White
February 2021
'Dudja' (Toodyay) 'Mist'

To all who sense something is radically wrong with economic, political and social systems in Australian society and want a better future that is good for all, contribute to each up and contribute whatever you are able to.

To my editor Hugh, publisher Carol, and the team at Coventry, thank you for your professional and personal assistance and support.

To you, my reader, thank you for being interested and engaged in the issues contained herein. Let all who do up and together make this wonderful country ...

John White
February 2021
Durdij (?Zoodjev), Dubai

Introduction

I love Australia! I count myself extremely fortunate to have been born in a resource-rich, climatically-agreeable, minimally-populated country where no one is shooting at me, the political and legal systems provide reasonable security for me, and I have freedoms and benefits that are the right of every human being. Unfortunately, not every citizen in Australia is as well-off as I am. I was born to a 'white, middle-class' family in a small, friendly town in a pleasant, rural region. Not every citizen enjoys such freedoms and benefits. Not every citizen enjoys the freedoms and benefits meant for all human beings.

There are citizens here who have not been accepted as such; who have been excluded from the beginning of colonial occupation of this land. Acknowledging the Ballardong Noongar Nation as original custodians of this South Western part of the land in which I was born is just a beginning. We need to *enact* that acknowledgment; the words are meaningless unless they are accompanied by wise, compassionate and resolute, restorative-justice in action.

A growing cohort of citizens are being increasingly marginalised by the systems under which Australia has been, and is, operating. The freedoms and benefits are being concentrated in the hands of fewer of our total number. And even they are not really free. The benefits that come from economic abundance have little to do with true freedom; freedom to be fully human, valuing integrity, equality and dignity for all people. Australia is not yet 'fair'; although on many measures we are ahead of many other countries, Australia is a long way from being fair!

Our major errors include the following: although there are great benefits from our association with the United Kingdom, we inherited the partisan political and economic systems of the privileged aristocracy, and we are modelling ourselves largely on the United States of America and, with them, degenerating on many issues of human significance. We are tending increasingly towards the 'rights' of the individual rather than those of the community. *'Because you're worth it!'* the advert states. We are becoming less fair to each other; less honourable towards each other. Crimes of violence are increasing in number and severity. Government is becoming less fair to the majority of citizens for whom government exists. We are becoming less fair to our neighbouring nations and to others throughout the world who need our support. We are richly resourced, yet are reducing our aid to poorer nations.

As individuals, we are encouraged by seductive advertising and ready availability of goods and services to spend first on ourselves – often for 'wants' that are well beyond our needs for a comfortable life. Many more of us don't have the basic provisions for such comfort and dignity. Our systems and the ethos that spawned and sustains them militate against fairness for all.

As civilizations develop over time, history demonstrates an inexorable 'growth to decline' in almost all of them. They begin with frontiers being discovered – or, more accurately, rediscovered – by a group of adventurers who share general equality of personal resources and have much in common. As communities grow and develop, skills and opportunities differentiate one from another. Wealth and influence are accumulated, and their distribution begins to become inequitable. With that shift, the 'freedoms and benefits' which are the right of all are lost to an increasing number of community members. With the increasing inequity, deepening poverty lives uncomfortably with wealth, discontent rises, desperation builds, violence emerges, groups and individuals wall themselves off for protection, factions array themselves against each other, and the end result is often revolution of some kind – usually destructive of people and property. This crazy cycle has been going on for thousands of years. We don't seem to learn.

There are notable exceptions, however. Indigenous nations throughout history, quarantined for a time from influences of imperialism, have managed to sustain their existence for millennia. Arguably the finest example is that of the Australian First Nations people – the Aborigines – who have lived in relative harmony with themselves and this land they occupied for upwards of 60,000 years. In the pages to come, we will consider key characteristics that supported such cultural longevity. If we are careful in that consideration, if we are sufficiently humble and willing to listen to and learn from it, if we have the courage to act on it, we may yet prevent a catastrophic collapse of all the good we know to exist in this great country to which we are privileged to belong.

There is great potential here. Great potential in each one of us. 'Hope' is one of the ingredients in the attainment of that potential! Knowing something of the amazing complexity, depth and *wonder* of the human being, I am hopeful. Hopeful that we will wake up, look for and learn from the goodness in life wherever it is to be found in the world. There are countries ahead of Australia on certain measures of community wellbeing. And there is a need for great wisdom, humility and courage if we are to realise the potential that can provide the freedoms and benefits that are the right of every human being.

Hope has two companions, *faith* and *love*. Each of us hopes for good. Each of us has faith – belief – of some description. Some of the things we believe in aren't working too well for us. That can change. And, most importantly, each of us has an inbuilt desire to receive and give love. There is more good news than bad if only we will seek it with 'all our heart, soul, mind and strength'. If that sounds like a spiritual exercise, that's because it is! For life to be good for all and for any individual, it has to be inclusive of our complete humanity – especially our deepest essence of the mystery we refer to as 'spirit or soul'. Dismissing any aspect of ourselves doesn't make sense. In fact, dismissing any aspect of ourselves actually makes trouble for us; the trouble we see all around the world.

Because we've either dismissed or diminished the focus on the deeper aspects of our humanity, we've allowed some fatal flaws to creep into the way we live life and where we place our value. This book is about becoming aware of a few of the major flaws in the way this country has been and is being run – how much of the world is being run, actually – and about how we might return to more of the good and less of the bad. And there *is* more of the good! And 'good' actually requires less effort to achieve. Why? Because 'good' is our common nature; our essence! We've just allowed ourselves to be derailed somewhat by intellectual cleverness that has been disguised as 'right and good for us'.

Before we look at how to get back to that 'good' – how to 'wake up' – let's first have a brief motivator; a reminder of the 'bad' from which we would like to – and need to – escape.

Life is coming apart at the seams. We see the disintegration all around us. The statistics on crime and deprivation justify the claim that the social institutions and processes that are supposed to unite us are in an advanced stage of decomposition. People have lost hope, which is why there has been the mass withdrawal from participation in politics... we observe the manifestations of disintegration every day in the destruction of life within the individual building blocks that make up society: the family. That is why... the biographical proclivities that 'explain' the aberrant actions of individuals count for little. Society is failing to nurture people... (who) sense that the origins of the problem stem from some fatal flaw 'in the system', a flaw which they intuitively believe must be fundamental because it has the power to threaten our living environment: Mother Earth. And yet, despite the evidence, our ideology inhibits us from acknowledging the reality; which is why many of the acts of self-destruction are interpreted as failures of the individual rather than expressions of something seriously wrong with the structure and function of society itself.

(Fred Harrison in *Corruption of Economics*, London: Shepheard-Walwyn, 1994, pp. 165-6.)

And the earth itself is tired. Very tired. It's languishing, bowed to almost breaking point by the pressure we humans are exerting on it, on all its amazing life forms, and on each other. Some are arguing that there are too many of us. That may be the case and something we need to consider as we endeavour to solve the problems mostly of our creation. It would seem that we are too clever for our own good and for the good of the earth. Of course, we humans, too, are inextricably part of nature, yet too few realise and live that reality. We are not separate from nature; we are made of the same elements of which earth is made. And the universe, for that matter. The trouble is also that we differ in some ways from all other life forms.

The major difference is the fact that we have a different *consciousness* from other creatures. Some will argue we are the *only* conscious species. Whatever the case, our consciousness is both a 'blessing and a curse.' The blessing enables us to think, to imagine, to dream, to be aware of ourselves, and to co-create with the Creator of all that is. That same reality is also a curse; it tempts us to think that, being different – being so-called 'superior' to other creatures – we are separate from nature. It tempts us to think that, being at the top of the food chain, we are in control. Even of nature. That nature is there for us to use as we so desire and with impunity.

A serious part of the 'curse' is that, because of our superior abilities, we can produce materials and substances that don't appear naturally on earth and are, therefore, unable to be recycled in the normal ways of nature. In our cleverness, we produce waste. Lots of it! Nature doesn't! Nature recycles everything, the entire eco-sphere interacting harmoniously and sustainably. We produce waste that the planet can't easily – can't even – deal with. We risk drowning ourselves in our own waste. And drowning or destroying countless other life forms in the process. There are vast islands of plastic bottles and other plastic waste forming in our oceans. Sea life is ingesting and becoming entangled in our waste. A recent report calculated that in a few years there will be more pieces of plastic in the oceans than there are fish! Our beaches and parks and roadways and waterways are clogged with plastic and other non-natural materials. And nano-particles of plastic are threatening the health of life forms in ways of which we, as yet, have limited understanding.

For several decades, science has been telling us that we are running out of time to stop the rot. We're running out of time to fix the damage we've done in order that life on earth – perhaps the life of the earth – can continue. We know that the burning of fossil fuels is producing atmospheric waste – CO_2 – that has changed the temperature of the planet, and is dislocating life forms that have been inhabiting certain regions for aeons. We know that alternative, affordable renewable energy resources are readily available and plentiful. Some farming practices – particularly in the West – are also emitting atmosphere-damaging gases. Many of us probably need to change our dietary demands. The circulation of ocean currents is changing, dramatically altering the distribution of solar energy from equatorial regions. Oceans are acidifying. Ice caps are melting reducing earth's fresh water storage, deforming the habitats of land, air and sea life, raising sea levels and displacing communities of humans and other creatures. Deserts are heating up, expanding, and reducing habitable areas for a multitude of life-forms. Forests that sequester CO_2 are being destroyed at an alarming rate simply to provide short-term profit for the few corporate entities with the power to claim their ownership. Economic survival is the driver of the destruction for others; the poor and marginalised. Rainfall is decreasing in some regions and dramatically increasing in others. Severe weather events are increasing in frequency and intensity, causing widespread destruction of natural and human-made infrastructure, causing floods, droughts and wild-fires, and dislocating whole communities of people and other creatures.

Unsurprisingly, people the world over are aware of the changes around them, and the negative impacts upon their livelihoods and lifestyles. Change causes anxiety; fear. And fear causes humans (and other creatures) to seek safety. One strategy is to return to the familiar. This can be seen in the tendency to *tribalisation*, strengthening of personal and national identities, borders and finances.

Safety in numbers. Safety at home. *'Make America great again'*, *'The future is for patriots'*, *'Look after number one'*, *'God bless Australia'*. Fear also causes other reactions. Often not well thought through. Sometimes violent. Military coups, violent demonstrations, physical attacks on minority groups or individuals, vilification of anyone who is 'different from me', extremism of all kinds. Fear. Fear for my personal survival or well-being.

How did humankind get to this disturbing place? How did we create the mess we and the planet are in? And, arguably more importantly, how can we fix the mess? Can we fix it? That would be good news, right? Well, I am pleased to say that all is not (yet) lost! There *is* good news!

What about this good news?

We have at our disposal – both individually and communally (and we need to value both of those realities equally) – gifts and talents, abilities and skills, knowledge and experience, historical precedents, internal and external qualities *absolutely up to the task* of realising the insanity in how we've been living, returning to our right minds (and, thus, spirits), repairing the damage, and co-creating ways of being human that work for each one of us and for all our earthly companions, crucially including flora, fauna, and the soil communities!

There is no utopia. But there is 'good enough' life for all. We are created for abundant life and have been freely given an abundant ecosphere. Considering the suffering that is unfortunately all too common for far too many people, it might be surprising to realise that our true identity – our central and deepest nature – is bliss! That's right! Sensible philosophy and religion, wisdom from many sources throughout history agree that, at our core, we are love and joy and peace; bliss! The deep reality of *shalom* (wholeness in every sense) is our source and destiny. The harmonious, tranquil, just, non-dual 'truth' is who we are; inwardly and outwardly if we simply, humbly submit to it.

If that statement seems outlandish to us, it's probably because we haven't experienced that *central nature* as often as we would like, to the extent that we would like, or maybe not even at all if our circumstances have demanded every grain of our attention and effort merely to take the next breath. To the shame of us so-called *enlightened* humans in the nations of the *haves*, such circumstances could have, and should have, never been allowed to occur to our suffering sisters and brothers. That suffering is one part of the insanity we've managed to accommodate and the possible reversal of which we'll be discussing in these pages.

In my recent book, *Uncommon Sense; reclaiming humanity* (Coventry Press, 2019), I set out what much wisdom literature generally accepts as the necessary foundation for considering how life on earth became dysfunctional, and how it may be healed and transformed. In the pages to come, I will briefly revisit some key points in that foundation as they relate to the themes of this book. In this review, I hope to expose and demonstrate how we have unwittingly abrogated personal responsibility and deferred to the thinking and values of our *ego-self*, and that of others, instead of accessing our own, formidable abilities as profound spiritual, moral, ethical beings. In doing so, we have allowed great damage to be done to ourselves, each other, and all the amazing creatures and life forms of planet earth.

All the information we need in order to make decisions about life is available to us! Lived experience, intuition, wisdom literature, scientific and technical information, experts, internet, etc. For those of us who are less able to access information, there is always someone who can assist if we ask. If we make ourselves available to humankind – open to life – every assistance required will be provided. Whatever opportunities are available, we can access them. Whatever damage has been done, in cooperation with the earth and with each other, we can repair it – as long as we don't delay any further! And we are the agents of repair! Of course, with any great endeavour, there are great requirements for success to be achieved. We have the requirements within ourselves; the qualities of intelligence, memory, spirit and will. The only question is will we submit to the discipline of employing those qualities to pursue true knowledge, justice and the common good, and acquire and express the wisdom, grace and courage necessary to heal ourselves and the earth?

Much in our educating and socialising systems has come to focus on less-than-completely who we are as human beings. Even our universities are tending to be more like trade schools, equipping students for specific societal roles, rather than teaching them how to *wake up*; to be; to think effectively, i.e. choose what to think about and focus our minds upon, discern wisely. Of course, for disciplines including medicine, engineering, and others, training in specific technical knowledge and skill is crucial.

But, alongside that, and to produce mature human beings to function in such roles, there is much room for the development of the spiritual, moral, existential aspects of being human.

Perhaps we can call this *deep thinking*; thinking with *all* of ourselves; our heart, soul, mind and strength. Leading us to experience the mysterious reality of our true nature which is argued by wisdom to be the Spirit of Love. Gentleness. Inclusion. Generosity. Compassionate, creative, dynamic, visionary, unifying Love, and all the practicalities that automatically follow from that. Practical, functional, *fair* economics and politics. Practical, functioning, *fair* social organisation. Principles of justice. Of equity.

Seeing correctly, we can think correctly, and act correctly. We can revisit the ways we interact with our sisters and brothers of our global humanity, with the creatures with whom we share the earth, with the systems of politics, economics and social organisation we have created. We can assess what adjustment is needed, and plan and enact the necessary repair and reorganisation. We will see the impact of the materials we create and use.

Seeing correctly, we will see the processes and dynamics underpinning the inequity in the way we view and treat each other, and distribute the wealth provided by the earth free to all creatures. We will see that we are inextricably one with the earth and all its inhabitants, that no person has greater worth than any other person. No person has superior right to material benefits. No person is to have control of any other person. No person is to be left behind, disregarded, disadvantaged or discarded by any other person or system. No person is to be used or abused for the pleasure of another. No person is to suffer indignity at the hands of another person or system.

We will see that gentleness rather than violence is true strength. And we will see everything as an opportunity for growth – not as politicians generally speak of growth purely in economic and technological terms – but, specifically, growth of humanity, community and without sacrificing the beauty of unique and invaluable individuality and our earth home. We will see fairness for all without the disadvantages and indignities of a welfare mentality. Nothing worth anything to lose; everything worth anything to gain! We will see the correct *sequence* of activity for life to function effectively; we will seek *righteousness first – justice* – and experience all other necessary things being added to us as a result of that priority.

Any adventure, any foray into the unknown or unusual, is generally exciting, challenging and often anxiety-producing – at least at first. But once commenced, and we realise that we're not going to self-destruct, anxiety is usually displaced by the euphoria of a new and fulfilling life experience. We are alive in a way we haven't known before. All is very well! As we wake up and think more deeply and effectively, as we begin to live as intended and desired, as we enter into the fullness of who we are, life in all its fullness works better than anything we have before known. As we wake up and responsibly bring our amazing abilities to bear on how life should be, we will see where we've missed the truth and be able to return to a path that works for all life.

We've seen systems of national organisation come and go throughout history. Some last longer than others. Kingdoms of one kind or another rise and fall with predictable regularity and great destruction and suffering. Communism has failed. Socialism has failed. Capitalism has failed. We are told by the few who designed capitalism that it is the only practical system. Those desperate few – who benefit disproportionately from capitalism – have historically gone to great lengths to ensure that nothing challenges their profit-taking. And, as can be seen by the increase in poverty and misery for the many alongside the increase in wealth and comfort for the decreasing few, they are manifestly wrong in their approach.

They have continually lied to us until we have accepted their lies as truth. Capitalism with its present arrangements of finance and markets, private ownership of vast resources, legal tax avoidance by the 'rent takers' is NOT the best and, therefore, only system. Another arrangement – eminently fair and sustainable – has been available for several hundred years. But, because it removes absolute control of wealth from the few whom that wealth benefits, it has been, and is, vigorously resisted and its proponents vilified; labelled 'Communist' or 'Socialist'. Because it allows for equitable sharing of power and opportunity, together with appropriate environmental preservation and sustainable land use, it is resisted. Because it calls time on pure human greed and promotes equity, it is resisted by the tiny and decreasing minority who benefit from it.

A word needs to be said here that, apart from this 'paradigm waiting in the wings for the past 250 years', for more than 60,000 years, an egalitarian system of life has been in practice right here in Australia.

In the pages to come, we will investigate the basic and fatal flaws in Neo-Classical Economic theory and practice, in current 'party politics' and, thus, in social organisation and public finance. This investigation has been written about throughout the last 250 years. But, because of the effective resistance to, and silencing of, its common sense and simplicity, it needs to be aired again. Insanity is doing the same thing and expecting a different outcome. Governments throughout the world are 'doing the same thing'; basing their financial management on fatally-flawed theories and practices. Developing nations are being 'assisted'– often through 'too-attractive-to-refuse' financial incentives and deals by so-called developed nations – to base their development on the same fatally-flawed systems that are perpetuating huge profits for the few and burgeoning poverty and abject misery for the many – not to mention the mindless, wholesale destruction of the eco-systems that support all life on earth.

I wonder if *uncommon sense* can be reignited for the benefit of all inhabitants of the planet; perhaps even to actually ensure the future of the planet.

As I stated at the outset, **I love Australia!** It's still one of the very best and safest countries in the world. Most of us for whom Australia is home are still the luckiest people in the world. But an increasing number are not lucky. Australia is not as *fair* as many of our leaders would have us believe. Perhaps it seems fair for them, because they breathe the rarefied air of privilege, wealth and power. But it's not as fair as it needs to be and could be if only we would make a couple of challenging but essential, radical, ethical changes; changes facilitated by our waking up to the reality that *Love* – our inner design – is to be the central factor in deciding our policies of economics, politics and social organisation for life to be truly *fair* for all.

Chapter 1

Unfair Economics

s I briefly alluded to in my recent book, *Uncommon Sense; reclaiming humanity* (Coventry Press, 2019), there are some deceitful, deliberate fatal flaws in the arrangement of the Neo-Classical Economics of today. In his profoundly insightful, controversial book, *Progress and Poverty* (1879), Henry George restated the basics of economic theory. He noted the three factors involved: *land, labour and capital*. Those same three factors remain, and always will, the fundamentals of economics. He pointed out the fatal flaw in the way those factors are manipulated by Neo-Classical Economists to interact such that they primarily benefit the few who hold land and its resources in private property.

The 'fatal flaw'

The fatal flaw is that *land* has been conflated with *capital*.

Because of its absolutely pivotal role in the effective functioning of justice in economic management, that fact is worth repeating. Land has been conflated – amalgamated

24

– with *capital*! This amalgamation has paved the way for monopolistic privatisation of public resources, and gross inequity in wealth distribution!

This deliberate and fatal aberration cannot be overstated. *Land* has come to be considered *capital* thus reducing to *two* the *three* fundamental elements in economics, thereby rendering economics corrupted and unworkable. For functional economics to exist, the three essential components of *land*, *labour* and *capital* must be allowed to retain their unique, unencumbered, un-enmeshed, individual functions in their interaction with one another.

It began to go wrong in the bronze age, 4000 years ago, when people embarked on a path of cultural diversification that is now impossible to sustain. They developed a set of social institutions and processes that have separated, on a systematic basis, the people from the land. Not everyone was thus alienated from his or her territorial roots, but the customarily thinkable principle – that it was possible to tolerate the inequality of rights of access to land –was accepted. Falteringly, at first; but accepted, slowly transformed into what we have today: a blind acceptance of the correctness of exclusive ownership of the benefits of land. This unnatural prejudice – unnatural because anti-evolutionary, in the Darwinian sense – was legitimised by convention and law, through Greece, Rome and its later medieval manifestations in Western Europe.

(Fred Harrison in *The Corruption of Economics*, London: Shepheard-Walwyn, London 1994, p. 10.)

If there seems anything strange in the idea that all men have equal and inalienable rights to the use of the earth, it is merely that habit can blind us to the most obvious truths'... 'nothing is more repugnant to the natural perceptions of men than that land should be treated as subject to individual ownership, like things produced by labour' ...' in every essential, land differs from those things which, being the product of human labour are rightfully property. 'Land' is the creation of God; they are produced by man'.... 'what more preposterous than that we... grant our own people or foreign capitalists the right to strip of their earnings citizens of the next generation'...

(Henry George, *Poverty and Progress*, 1879)

That is the fatal flaw in Neo-Classical Economics (N.C.E). Private ownership of land and its resources removes access for all people to the benefits of that land; access to a living of dignity and adequacy. Unless and until that is reversed, all economic management will ever do is fiddle around the peripheries of fiscal and public finance matters. Nothing of any significance will be achieved in terms of producing justice, truth and the public good, the primary qualities of democracy; inequitable distribution will remain entrenched and the entrenchment will worsen. Deepening poverty for an increasing number of citizens will reside increasingly uncomfortably with increasing wealth for the diminishing few who have immorally, unethically but legally - bought and own the 'game'.

How did this fatal flaw come about? Montesquieu provides a guide: '*In the birth of societies, it is the chiefs of the republic who frame the institutions, and afterwards it is the institutions which mould the chiefs of the republic*' (*Rousseau, The Social Contract, Wordsworth Editions, 1998, p. 40*). The 'chiefs' who framed our western nations were 'guided' (manipulated may be a more accurate term) by men of money and power. They ensured that institutions were

26

legislated in such a way that their personal interests were protected, and that inequality – whether intended or not – would be the guaranteed outcome. There are, of course, many in our world who actually believe that some men have greater right to privileged life than others; these deluded souls have been 'conditioned' by centuries of aristocratic classism.

A telling example is in the original wording of the American Declaration of Independence, first drafted by Thomas Jefferson. *'We hold these truths to be sacred and unalienable; that all men are created equal and independent, that from that equal creation they derive rights inherent and unalienable, among which are the preservation of life, liberty and property.'* After a committee of five did some edits, the final version reads *'We hold these truths to be self-evident, that all men are created equal, that they are endowed by their Creator with certain unalienable Rights, that among these are Life, Liberty and the pursuit of happiness.'*

Somewhere in that process, the institution was created ensuring that *pursuit of happiness* replaced *access to property.* Intended or not, from that point, it became possible for inequality to flourish, and for some to acquire much property whilst others had to be content to 'pursue happiness' the best way they could in the unequal arena. Because of lack of access to the very thing required for happiness, i.e., satisfaction of basic human needs for a dignified life, that 'pursuit' of happiness was doomed to frustration and failure from the start. The fatal flaw enshrined in law!

In living memory, because land has always been treated as 'capital asset', we might say 'what's the problem'? Henry George has an answer that passes scientific scrutiny, and that we will discuss in the following pages.

Land, labour and capital

Land is needed to produce capital. Capital, in the first instance, is dependent upon, and is produced by, labour exerting effort on land (including water and air). In a beginning society, there is only *land* and *labour*. There is equality, cooperation, sharing of resources of food and skills, etc. Wealth is produced. *Capital* is born! As the society develops and 'matures', those with the capital automatically assume the authority and 'right' to exert influence on the development of systems that organise the society. Central to those systems is the 'rule' by which the resources of land are accessed. As the *majority without capital* are dependent for their existence upon those *with* capital, that *authority* and those '*rights*' are not effectively challenged, and so they pass into common practice.

As a consequence, the unchallenged authority evolves into the system in which those with 'capital authority' become the ones who make and sustain the laws to which all are then subject; laws that favour the law-makers and not the majority of citizens! One of those laws – arguably the most sinister and the very foundation of inequity – is that law legislating the private 'ownership' and appropriation of earth's resources for the personal use of the 'appropriator'. Capital enables the 'capitalist' to acquire and hold as private property a greater proportion of the land and its resources for his personal use, and from which to personally benefit. When land is held in private ownership, the benefits of that land are no longer available for any other citizen.

Additionally, as the productivity or potential worth of a piece of land increases its value, those seeking land to produce a livelihood are forced to pay increasingly for that right – either to purchase from the owner, or to pay a rent to the owner. The amount of available land is finite. Demand increases its value, putting it beyond the financial means of an increasing number of citizens. Recently, the Australian Prime Minister infamously stated, '*if you have a go, you get a go*'! What he didn't acknowledge was that under present rules of ownership, it is impossible for the majority to '*have a go*'! The only ones to '*get a go*' are the few who make and sustain the rules of the game, and who hold the wealth and power.

Jean-Jacques Rousseau famously stated that '*man is born free and everywhere he is in chains*' (*The Social Contract*, Wordsworth Editions, U.K, 1998, p. 5). Man (and woman and child) is in chains for several reasons. Here, we are considering the economic chains manufactured and attached by the patently evil system that has put land – which was provided by God freely for all creatures – in private ownership. For Rousseau, private ownership of more property than supplies one's needs is to be disallowed. '*Every man has by nature a right to all that is necessary to him; but the positive act which makes him proprietor of certain property excludes him from all the residue. His portion having been allotted, he ought to confine himself to it, and he has no further right to the undivided property*' (ibid, p. 21).

For any citizen to produce personal wealth, they must have access to land and its resources on which to exert their labour. Because of private property in land, values continue to increase making it ever-more difficult for everyone to access land on which they can labour and build for their personal well-being. Associated with this trending reality is that wealth automatically becomes ever-more concentrated in the hands of fewer and fewer individuals, and the gulf between the wealthy and the poor widens and deepens. Human nature is such that increasing wealth is seductive. It often brings with it a (misguided) sense of power and worth as a person. The ordinariness and equality of the human person is distorted, creating a psychological barrier between wealthy and non-wealthy, and producing fertile ground for the destructive development of mistrust and fear, resentment and isolation, pride and envy, and all manner of anti-social behaviour.

To focus on what is external to the person – for example, their wealth – breeds an unhealthy valuing of, and reliance on, material 'stuff'. Wealth acquisition and protection absorb one's attention and energies, and the deeper, profound, sacred human reality – the soul or spirit that generates equality, justice, mercy and compassion – is lost to awareness and function of the person and, thus, to the community at large. Greed emerges. One of the seven deadly sins! In her disturbingly-revealing book, *Capitalism: a Ghost Story* (Haymarket books, U.S. 2014), Booker Prize winner, Arundhati Roy, gives us one story of untrammelled excess in the midst of unconscionable poverty and suffering. She described the dwelling of India's then-richest man, Mukesh Ambani. The 'home' had twenty-seven floors, three helipads, nine lifts, hanging gardens, ballrooms, weather rooms, gymnasiums, six floors of parking, six hundred servants, and a twenty-storey-high wall of lawn attached to a vast metal grid. She made the point that *'the grass was dry in patches and bits had fallen off in neat rectangles. Clearly, trickle-down hadn't worked'* (p. 7). She noted, though, that *'Gush-Up'* works as *'in a population of 1.2 billion, India's one hundred richest people own assets equivalent to one-fourth of the GDP'*, (ibid). *'According to the rules of the Gush-Up Gospel, the more you have the more you can have'... It's a dream come true for businessmen – to be able to sell what you don't have to buy'* (ibid, p. 9).

The problem of greed

Greed distorts humanity and destroys life.

Greed separates and isolates one from one's deepest Self, from others and from creation; from the natural environment from which all life springs and is sustained.

Greed denies the possibility of justice, truth and the public good.

Of course, wealth is not greed. Wealth – capital – is benign, useful and necessary if employed correctly. Used correctly, wealth builds up and integrates; used incorrectly, it tears down and isolates. Our present system of N.C.E is fatally flawed, because it was designed and has been sustained by the tiny minority and for their personal gain. In reality, it has been for their personal loss; loss of soul; loss of a common humanity of justice, truth, compassion, equity, peace. This system of inequitable access to, and distribution of, the wealth produced by the majority who labour, is fatally flawed and must be transformed if humankind is to survive with any degree of dignity and maturity, and if all other life forms are to survive and sustain the delicate balance of the ecosphere. The present system on which we have relied for generations is broken beyond repair.

> Capitalism is as redundant as the social system built on the communist ideology. The world needs a new paradigm. Such a paradigm does exist. It has been lurking like a ghost in the literature of scholars and artists for over 200 years. It could be called by one of many names, but the label that economists and historians would recognise would be 'the Georgist paradigm', after the American social reformer, Henry George (1839-1897). Over the past century, attempts to transform Henry George's central idea into social reality have been made by men of action like Winston Churchill and sensitive artists like Leo Tolstoy; but to no avail. The force of unreason was overwhelmingly against them'.
>
> (Fred Harrison in *The Corruption of Economics*, London: Shepheard-Walwyn, London 1994, p. 167.)

In fact, the list of supporters of the Georgist paradigm that promotes public ownership of land and resources is impressive. We would be arrogant in the extreme to dismiss these thinkers and others like them. That's exactly what we're doing! The list includes Mark Twain (1835-1910), John Stuart Mill (1806-1873, English philosopher), Clyde Cameron (1913-2008, Minister in the Australian Whitlam Government and UN General Assembly delegate), James Lalor (1807-1849, Irish independence and justice advocate), Sun Yat Sen (1866-1925, father of Chinese economic revolution), Walter Burley Griffin, 1876-1937 (designer of Canberra),

Aldous Huxley, 1894-1963, (acclaimed novelist, philosopher and environmentalist), Banjo Paterson, 1879-1941, (Australia's great poet), Albert Einstein, 1879-1955,(physicist, philosopher), Helen Keller, 1880-1968, (deaf, blind, tireless American reformer), David Lloyd George, (1863-1945, British Prime minister), John Locke, 1632-1704, (English pioneer of economic liberalism), William Penn, 1644-1718, (Quaker founder of Pennsylvania), Benjamin Franklin, 1706-1790, (statesman, abolitionist, co-drafter of American Declaration of independence, U.S. President), Thomas More, 1478-1535, (English lawyer, writer and politician who opposed the extension of power of Henry VIII and was beheaded for his efforts), Jean-Jacques Rousseau, 1712-1778, (brilliant philosopher and champion of 'Liberté, Fraternité, Egalité' long before the French Revolution), Abraham Lincoln, 1809-1865, (acclaimed US President and man for the people), Voltaire, 1694-1778, (one of France's greatest writers and philosophers), George Orwell, 1903-1950, (well-known and admired English writer, author of *Animal Farm*), Thomas Jefferson 1743-1826, (author of the American Declaration of Independence and third US President), Adam Smith, 1723-1790, (author of *The Wealth of Nations*, one of the most important works on economics ever written), George Bernard Shaw, 1856-1950, (Irish Nobel Prize in literature and Oscar winner), Alfred Deakin, 1857-1919, (one of the fathers of Australian Federation and three times Prime Minister of Australia), Mikhail Gorbachev, (leader of the Soviet Union and Nobel Peace laureate), Chief Seattle, 1786-1866, (Great Native-American leader, embodiment of nobility and speech)... the list goes on and includes Chaim Weizman, Teddy Roosevelt,

Bill Mollison, Franz Oppenheimer, Joseph Stiglitz, Charles Darwin and more. ('*Georgists in History*' – paper by Karl Williams).

With fervent support by such an august group, why has the new paradigm been sidelined, we might ask? Greed for wealth and power is the short answer. The minority group called landowners and 'rent-takers' do not want to relinquish their power and some of their excess wealth. I say 'excess' because, by the laws they themselves have made and sustain, they have appropriated for their personal use *the resources of the earth that were freely given by God for the benefit of all creatures* (Henry George, *Progress and Poverty*, 1879).

The reader may be interested to research the antecedents of 'Georgism', that included philosophers like Quesnay, Turgot, Adam Smith and others dating from 17th century. For the purposes of brevity and practicality here, we confine our focus to the thinking of Henry George, who drew inspiration from these early philosophers, distilled their contributions of wisdom, and articulated a simple, ethical, workable model of synthesis.

The Georgist Paradigm

But what of capitalism? It limps along, with its principal spokesmen – political leaders from the richest industrial nations, civil servants representing the world financial institutions – plaintively pleading for unity behind a single set of policies. They hope that these policies, an unconvincing matrix drawn from failed experiments of the past, will bail the global economy out of the depression of the 1990s and set the world on a new course to sustainable prosperity. We are persistently told by the apologists that the capitalist paradigm offers the best arrangement mankind can devise. This claim is undermined by the Georgist paradigm, whose critique of the old system begins the process of illuminating the vision of a qualitatively different kind of society.

(Fred Harrison in *The Corruption of Economics*, London: Shepheard-Walwyn, London 1994, p. 168.)

How can we be confident that a new paradigm can be taken seriously?

First, to be of value, the new paradigm must be able to identify the fatal flaws in the existing systems. The strengths of the Georgist paradigm expose the weaknesses at the heart of capitalism and communism.

Second, the Georgist paradigm offers an approach to life that appears to synchronise with people's overriding aspirations. For example, it rejects coercion and offers liberty, and it is able to specify precisely how this state of freedom can be achieved for everyone. In other words, it makes sense to ordinary folk.

Third, the paradigm specifies the mechanism for executing two crucial tasks: (i) it explains how to facilitate the transition to a new society without the use of force... (ii) the governing mechanism offered by the new paradigm is self-sustaining.

Fourth, the economic pillars of the paradigm can be described in rigorously testable terms. This means (in the language of the scientist) that they can, in principle, be falsified. The paradigm, therefore, is a scientifically based theory. In the past century all tests have failed to discredit the theory.

Fifth, the foundations of the paradigm are grounded in both a morality and an anthropological tradition that are unassailable.

(*Fred Harrison in* The Corruption of Economics, *London: Shepheard-Walwyn, London 1994, p. 168-9.*)

These economic principles emphasising a reform of public finance have been known for 250 years in Europe, and were articulated originally by the physiocrats in 18th century France (Quesnay, Turgot et al), echoed in a *seminal treatise of economics'* by Adam Smith (*The Wealth of Nations*, 1776, and further developed in the 19th century culminating in *'the most comprehensive treatment from the pen of Henry George, a journalist in California, who wanted to know why poverty was an endemic feature of a society that enjoyed abundance of natural resources and wealth'* (Harrison, p. 170).

In the light of the overwhelming evidence for the Georgist Paradigm, the question we need to ask it 'why has it not been enthusiastically endorsed and brought into the mainstream of public finance? The answer, as mentioned earlier, is that it was and is 'opposed by the most powerful of all vested interests: the private owners of land,' who were not going to relinquish their *'status in society, which flowed from their command over the rental income of land...'* (Harrison) No-one should receive unearned income. It is neither fair to those who labour for their income, nor to the souls of those who do not.

Henry George recognised that the problem with society was simply the maldistribution of the benefits of land. Of course, he was not the first to make this observation. Since the birth of capitalism, innumerable anti-capitalist would-be reformers have observed similarly. The solution was to reform the system of public finance.

Problematic Taxation

Because of the flaw of land being conflated with capital, it has been necessary to devise ever-increasingly complex systems of taxation. And still there is an ever-increasing drive by government for more taxes from those who can least afford them 'to provide essential public services'. (A note on this matter shortly). Why the shortfall in taxes? Because the resource wealth that rightfully belongs to all citizens – to the public finances – is being privatised by a few who are growing obscenely rich at the cost of those from whom they are legally- but not ethically or morally – stealing. (Remember we spoke earlier about institutions being established by the rich and powerful to protect their personal interests?) If that situation isn't sufficiently 'unfair', governments often propose tax cuts for the wealthy on the erroneous belief that such an action boosts business which, in turn, boosts employment. History shows that it doesn't. Rather than spending their tax relief into the economy, the wealthy generally use it to pay down debt and add to their wealth by saving. But when tax cuts are provided to those on lower incomes – the majority of citizens, that much-needed money is mostly spent into the economy.

The 'Georgist' proposal had sensible, defensible things to say about taxation arrangements to fund the social requirements of the community. He proposed the implementation of a single tax; a tax on land. As land would no longer be held in private ownership, land would be 'rented' from the body of citizens who were its owners – or, better, *custodians*, for we all die but the land remains for those who come after us! Rent would be charged on the value of the resources existing in a particular parcel of land. Improvements produced on the land by the tenant would become the personal property of the tenant. Dwellings, factories, equipment, infrastructure, etc., would become personal property, but the land on which they are situated would be rented from the public in whose 'ownership/custodianship' it would remain in perpetuity.

From Australian mines, for example, each year billions of dollars become the personal wealth of the few private individuals who legally but immorally assume the right to personally benefit from public assets. Again, legally but immorally, miniscule royalties are returned to the public coffers, little or no tax is paid, and the public is denied the benefit of what was *given freely by God for the good of all* (Henry George, *Progress and Poverty*). The laws that make this inequity possible were, of course, created, legislated, implemented and sustained by the powerful and wealthy who are the primary beneficiaries.

Unless land is separated from capital, the decline of humankind and all life-forms on the whole earth will continue unabated. A new system must be developed and implemented. And it is possible. One of the oldest cultures on earth – that of the Australian Aborigines – is testament to that possibility. Based on a system of 'custodianship' rather than ownership, this culture has existed for something like 60,000 years. The custodianship arrangement enabled each member of their community group to revere the land, participate in its care, and benefit from it. Each person was involved with the husbanding of the land, maintaining its integrity, beauty, productivity. From such engaged, egalitarian involvement, each person gained a sense of appropriate significance and meaning. Depression and despair were unknown in such communities. Of course, as each person is unique and individual, differences were ever-present. Disagreements and conflicts occurred within and between groups, and were resolved in ways that generally reconciled recalcitrants to themselves and their communities rather than them being rejected and isolated in the way to which we in the west seem addicted.

Henry George travelled to several countries, including Britain and Australia, and spoke to crowds of people and many leaders, and his proposal was enthusiastically endorsed by most who heard him. As mentioned earlier, Britain's Lloyd George and Winston Churchill were two of many parliamentarians who supported the Georgist paradigm. In South Australia in 1933, an independent representative was elected to the South Australian parliament on the Georgist platform; and he represented an agricultural region of land-owners. And yet, support in abundance came from the very farmers whose land George was proposing *they would no longer own* but would rent on the basis of the land's productive benefit. These farmers could see that his single tax would provide adequately for society's service needs, disadvantage no citizen, and would result in all people retaining more of the benefit of their personal labours.

The new paradigm would see increased incentive for greater production because, after paying the appropriate rent for their land and its resources, *those who laboured would keep all remaining income from their labours;* there would be no income tax, provisional tax, sales tax, capital gains tax, GST, VAT or any other tax. The personal exertion of labour would become purposeful, personally beneficial and, thus, motivating and pleasurable. Such motivation would increase productivity, land locked up by speculators would be released and brought into production, wealth of all would increase, inequity would decrease, the obscenely rich would be less rich, poverty and crime would be dramatically reduced, all would be comfortable, mental, physical and social health would improve, all essential social services would be adequately financed by public funds, every local community would be humming predominantly with small and medium enterprises. Citizens could see that they would be financially and socially better off by renting the land on which they lived and worked, private ownership no longer being of any benefit. Of course, they still privately owned all the improvements, buildings, infrastructure, etc., and had security of tenure by agreement designed by the new paradigm. The details and the transition would be made over several years to avoid any sudden shock to trading and social arrangements.

Resistance

However, the minority group of powerful and wealthy – the rent-taking, capitalist property-owners – who were benefitting disproportionately from the resources that belonged to all citizens, effectively discredited the Georgist paradigm and saw it completely sidelined. They achieved this feat by becoming the paymasters of a new breed of economists. This Neo-Classical group redesigned economic theory and practice as we've discussed above, removing the 'land' factor – the third essential for the economic system to be workable – by conflating land with capital. Schools of Economics in prestigious American Universities were provided millions of dollars by industrialists and property owners to reset the fundamentals – the inviolable truths – of economic theory, thus rendering it corrupt.

The rest is history. We have inherited, and are blighted to this day, by the results of this truncation of sound economic theory. Accordingly, we have deepening and widening poverty in the midst of eye-watering wealth. We have the resources of nature, that are to be accessible to all citizens, privately owned by the few wealthy and powerful. The citizens are effectively denied access to the very elements of life that can make life liveable and beautiful; denied access to nature that is the free gift to all earth's inhabitants.

According to Henry George, private ownership of land must be abolished. The solution to removing poverty from the midst of great wealth could not be achieved any other way. In Australia, 'closing the gap' – or, more accurately, a 'gaping chasm' – between Non-Indigenous and Indigenous will not happen any other way! Our Aboriginal sisters and brothers have been removed from, and are still denied access to, the land which was, by birthright, theirs before it was ours! Whilst the abundance freely provided to be shared equitably by all could be personally appropriated by the few powerful members of society, justice, truth – fairness – will never be attained. Whilst foreign entities are permitted and encouraged to 'own' a nation's resources and carry on commerce internationally, their benefits protected by laws they proscribe, the people of the nation will receive no benefit from that commerce. *'Any branch of foreign commerce'*, says the Marquis d'Argenson, *'diffuses merely a deceptive utility through the kingdom generally; it may enrich a few individuals, even a few towns, but the nation as a whole, gains nothing, and the people are none the better for it'* (See Rousseau, *Social Contract*, p. 53).

System Change

In its present form, the Western economic system – the capitalist system of resource ownership by a diminishing few individuals – is broken beyond repair. Struggling to exist on or below the poverty line is the daily experience of an increasing number of Australians. For many, hope is waning. Despair is growing. Radical change must be achieved for economic and social justice to become a reality. Providentially, here in Australia we have a model for such change that has functioned in the Aboriginal society for around 60,000 years; an egalitarian model of societal organisation, economic well-being of all clans and individuals, and national land management closer to the concept and operation of democracy than any other in the history of humankind. More on that in the next chapter.

But, before we move on, back for a moment to the 'problematic taxation' section, and that *'note'* on the *'government drive for more taxes to provide essential services.'*

The Covid-19 pandemic tearing mercilessly through the world's population in 2020 is wreaking destruction of life rarely experienced. Hundreds of thousands have died. Millions are suffering loss of loved ones, are dislocated from normal life, separated from families and homelands, and no longer have livelihoods. Many businesses have closed, many will not recover. The loss of both social and material well-being is immeasurable. Whilst not wanting to sound callous, such devastation also brings opportunities for change: change to hopes, dreams and goals; change to how we value and care for each other; change to work practices and priorities; change to political, economic and social theories and practices.

I want to focus for a moment on change to various government's policy and action so far in this pandemic, and the possibilities of further and radically-transformative change if governments are willing to think outside their limiting, ideological boxes. The government policy of raising *'taxes to provide for essential services'* has been turned on its head. An obsession with 'budget surplus' has been reluctantly abandoned, and billions of dollars have been 'found' to provide necessary income support for the majority of Australians. The money 'found' has not been from taxes raised because, at present, the tax revenue has decreased. This 'found' money is nothing other than numbers on the Reserve Bank's balance sheet, and 'found' with a few key-strokes on a computer keyboard!

The reality is that, in a nation such as ours, in which we are fortunate to have a sovereign currency – an aspect of monetary policy which we must never abandon as many European nations have done to their detriment – our government cannot run out of money! *We can't run out of money*! Our government is a currency 'issuer' not a currency 'user' and the rules are dramatically different. You and I can't print and issue money – unless we want to spend time at Her Majesty's pleasure – and we have to *save* or *borrow* before we can *spend*. Our government is authorised to *issue* currency and can therefore *create* and *spend* before it *saves* (taxes) or *borrows*.

Politicians – especially the conservative side – are at present demonstrating the *exact opposite* of what they traditionally 'spin' to us, that we have to 'cut services because we can't afford them'. Clearly, they can and are affording essential support at present, and that is sensible, economically and socially responsible governance. However, because of an ideological and irrational fear of *big deficit*, more than 1.5 million citizens are being denied necessary support. The one issue that government ideology continues to incorrectly, incompetently promote is that *'the future generations will be saddled with a huge debt'*.

Modern Monetary Theory (MMT) has been around for decades, but has been misunderstood, vilified and dismissed by conservative, neo-classical economists. MMT refutes absolutely the assertion of *'huge future debt'*. As the so-called 'debt' is merely numbers on the Reserve Bank's balance sheet, that 'debt' can be eliminated with a few keystrokes on the same computer at the Reserve Bank. In times of crisis or hardship, nations with sovereign currency can spend whatever is needed to manage the downturn, as they are spending – and borrowing, if necessary, *from themselves* – in their own currency and, therefore, are in 'debt' to no-one. This facility, ably-implemented by the Government during the 2008 Global Financial Crisis, averted the worst of the crisis for Australia, and this strategy was acknowledged by a number of world leaders as sound economic management. President John Kennedy used deficit to land a man on the moon. Taxes didn't pay for it. Franklin Roosevelt used massive deficit spending to create more than ten million jobs in the 1930s after the Great Depression.

According to MMT, a government could and should ensure *zero unemployment* by introducing a 'Job Guarantee'; the unemployed becoming *government employees* occupied in real jobs in essential infrastructure development, and in the 'care economy' that would ensure optimum staffing in health and aged care, and all such social and essential services that produce a life of dignity and equity for all citizens. It is feasible that current, inadequate unemployment benefits could be transformed into guaranteed jobs with a *liveable wage*. The benefits to the community can be easily appreciated: provision of millions of hours of real service (productivity) to the community for money being spent, rather than zero hours of productivity being provided by those on unemployment benefits; a stable, psychologically and socially-healthy workforce, maintaining themselves and their dependents, each one contributing effectively to the well-being of the whole; finance being returned to the economy in the forms of spending, taxation and business confidence.

As the hard times pass and confidence and production in the private sector resurge, there is both an automatic flow of some workers from the public to the private sector (as demand for labour offers increased incentives) – a flow made easily because of the *maintained-employability* of workers previously on Job Guarantee – and an increase in revenue, steadily reversing government deficit.

Although Georgism maintains that a single tax on the benefits of land would be sufficient to provide for all the needs of a society, as the interdependent but uncoordinated economies of the world have become so complex and volatile, it is likely to be necessary in nations like ours to also use well-targeted taxes to balance supply and demand. MMT proponents suggest that, rather than providing for essential services, the major function of taxation is to manage inflation. In her insightful recent book *The Deficit Myth* (John Murray publishers, UK, 2020), author Professor Stephanie Kelton, an economic advisor to the U.S. Senate and acclaimed international speaker, wisely and skilfully presents a scenario of what government could achieve if freed from the 'myth' *that deficit is to be avoided because it is bad*. Kelton asserts that governments with sovereign currencies continue to function as 'currency users' rather than 'currency issue-ers'. In doing so, and in the interests of what they call 'efficiency', they seem to believe they need to cut essential public services in order to 'balance the budget'. Rather than a 'balanced budget', Kelton suggests that the focus of good government ought to be a 'balanced economy': monetary and fiscal policy ensuring adequate provision and meaningful occupation for all citizens; government 'effectiveness' rather than 'efficiency'.

In the 1940s, Abba P. Lerner, (Associate Professor, the Graduate Faculty of the New York School for Social

Research) coined the term 'functional finance', a macro-economic, 'economy-balancing' theory and practice ensuring the three major responsibilities of good government: avoidance of unemployment, avoidance of monopolistic control, and equitable distribution of wealth. In his book *The Economics of Control* (Macmillan, NY, 1944), Lerner spoke of the need for government not to abrogate responsibility for citizen welfare and allow it to be determined by the caprice of the capitalist market system. Here in Australia, and around the world, we are seeing the disasters of such abrogation. Lerner denied the 'principles' of both capitalism and collectivism, but accepted both as 'means' to be selectively and appropriately employed for the public good. Neither state dictatorship (absolute control) nor capitalist dictatorship (laissez faire) was to be embraced.

He observed that government-funded public welfare is both essential and paramount in effective governance and, combined with the instruments of the 'capital market system', could achieve the required functional financing of the nation. Lerner promoted a 'controlled economy' in which government dictated the 'means' of monetary and fiscal policy and practice, rather than allowing market forces to produce an 'uncontrolled economy': an economy of boom and bust cycles, privatisation of public resources, and inequitable distribution of national wealth.

It's on the public record that in the 2008 global financial crisis, the U.S Congress authorised a deficit of $787 billion requested by President Obama. Some of his advisors recommended at least $1.3 trillion was needed to avoid a protracted recession. According to Professor Kelton,

Obama, thinking like a 'currency user' rather than as a 'currency issuer', listened to other advisors, lost his nerve, and settled on the smaller deficit. The result was a decade of sluggish and painful recovery. In view of that, Kelton stated that *'bigger deficits would have enabled a faster and stronger recovery, protecting millions of families and avoiding trillions in income losses'* (ibid, p 8).

Australia now

Right now (late 2020) in Australia, we have a similar tragedy unfolding. The Government is functioning as a 'currency user', not as a 'currency issuer'; putting fear-based, arbitrary limits on government spending, rather than realising it has the capacity to spend *however much is needed* to stimulate and balance the economy; to maintain family incomes and livelihoods for *all* citizens; restore consumer confidence and sustain consumer spending; achieve a rapid and strong social and economic recovery. Even though the pandemic is severely complicating the function of Australian society at present, Government has the ability to ensure that no one is grossly disadvantaged, that social cohesion and security are maintained, and that an ordered, sound recovery is made into a society with improved quality of life for all. The Government is failing to adequately exercise that ability, and is ensuring a slow, post-Covid recovery. The greatest pain will be borne by those with the least resources and greatest need – the students, the aged, the unwell, the small and medium business proprietors, the ordinary 'Aussie battler'. The great, avoidable loss will be in the wicked waste of opportunity to rapidly increase essential infrastructure and human services to become a socially and economically healthy nation; leading the world in renewable energies technology; refining our mineral resources, manufacturing and exporting products produced by renewable energies, and even exporting renewable energy.

At the time of writing, the signs are not good. The Government seems wedded to fossil-fuel interests and associated environmental destruction, rejecting the advice of local and international experts on climate change and functional economics, and the common-sense views of an increasing majority of Australian citizens.

In a new book *Super Power* (2019), Australian economist and professional fellow of economics at University of Melbourne, Ross Garnaut, shows that using renewable energies, *'Converting one-quarter of Australian iron oxide and one half of aluminium oxide exports to metal would add more value and jobs than current coal and gas combined'* (p. 185). Employment, value and zero emissions by 2030 is available! Incomprehensively, not only is government rejecting the employment and value in movement away from gas, its obsession with a 'gas-led recovery', and its associated carbon emissions, directly contradicts government's stated commitment to *reduce* emissions.

The 'looming disaster' is, primarily, one of 'politicking', the focus of the next chapter.

Chapter 2

Unfair Politics

Together with the turmoil of grossly dysfunctional economics – and, arguably, because of it – there's also great turmoil in Australian politics. There has been for a very long time. Not only are parties fighting each other with unrelenting vigour and vitriol, they are fighting within their own parties. Internal divisions are more rife and wider than they ever have been. No matter how they are tweaked and massaged and members mollified, improvement in the party function seems unattainable. There seems to be a fatal flaw here too! Politicians look more like small children fighting for limited playthings than adult leaders of a nation. Yesterday, a colleague and I were watching a mob of sheep in a paddock adjacent to the Beverley Airstrip where our gliding operations were under way. I was on tow-pilot duty for the day and, between launches, we were chatting. There were two sheep in a stand-off, butting their heads together and backing off for a repeat of the contest. The rest of the mob were wandering disinterestedly away. My astute friend, Geoff, commented, *'There's a picture of Australian politics right there: the politicians mindlessly bashing each other and the rest of the Australian population wandering away in disgust!'*

The 'Party Flaw'

The party system of politics ensures the acquisition and maintenance of wealth and power for the minority of players who influence – 'direct and drive' might be more accurate – the policies and activities of the parties they support. This desire and design is one of personal self-gratification, including the acquisition of wealth, influence, power (or, the illusion of it) and, especially in the case of the conservative side of politics, various *particular* interests that often have little to do with the public good of a nation of citizens. On the Left side of politics, the interest is more likely to be for a greater proportion of the citizenry, but the party vehicle is still problematic for reasons we will shortly consider in this discussion.

Although conceived in order to govern a nation, the party system generally serves only minorities. That fact makes it undemocratic; it has little interest in, and commitment to, truth, justice and the public good – the hallmarks of democracy!

The way 'democratic' political parties operate has remained largely unchanged for hundreds of years. The vitriol, back-biting, back-stabbing, vilification, infighting, manipulation, outright lies and every other dysfunctional means of 'communication' (I use that term generously here), could make one wonder why we continue with such a structure that clearly lacks something significant. The current situation in Australia at least is that an increasing proportion of society is indicating that we don't want to continue with the present structure.

In his recent publication *Our Very Own Brexit* (Penguin 2019), Sam Roggeveen, Director of the Lowy Institute's International Security Program, writes of the move away from support of the major parties. He talks of political parties being withdrawn from their public bases, and of the voters' increasing disinterest in politicians and their parties generally, whilst maintaining and even increasing interest in the political issues of significance to them. Statistics demonstrate clearly that membership of major parties has declined dramatically over the past several decades in most Western democracies, including Australia.

Roggeveen correctly makes the point that during the Cold War, Australian parties had a reasonable degree of functional stability and bilateral purpose: supporting their allies, the US and UK, against the Soviet Communists. The Cold War ended and, with it, any sense of bi-partisanship. It is instructive that, when a nation's security is under threat, the entire leadership and citizens think and act as 'one' against the common enemy. The present Covid-19 pandemic paralysing the world at present is a case in point. Here in Australia, in the interests of the public good, political partisanship and associated ideology was abandoned, and a National Cabinet comprising state leaders of both 'sides' of politics was formed. For a few brief weeks, it functioned effectively as a single government, demonstrating that, when the public good is to be served – and should that not be always? – parties, sides are irrelevant. As the threat diminished, the old ideologies and dysfunctional partisanship returned.

Enjoying general support of both major parties, the deconstruction of the White Australia Policy heralded our embrace of multiculturalism. With multiculturalism no longer in question, no Cold War and now a declining U.S. ally and a rising China trading partner and neighbour, both parties have lost their *'raison d'etre'* and are floundering around trying to find a reason for being. They find themselves with no cause to provide focus and direction, and little to differentiate themselves from each other. The removal by unconscious bilateral agreement of the adversarialism of 'labour versus capital', has taken yet another focus from both major parties. Neither having found their 'purpose', their machinations of self-destruction, incoherent policies, and little idea of how to be or what to do, has resulted in political impotence and irrelevance. Sam Roggeveen says:

> As major political parties lost touch with their social and economic base, they also professionalised... became more closely tied to the state, their policies began to converge. Politicians from all major parties begin to form a separate class in which they have more in common with each other than with the party members and voters they are supposed to represent (*Our Very Own Brexit*, p. 23).

Rather than politicians being drawn from the public via their individual experience, understanding and personal authority to drive reform, they now come to politics generally via the path of university-politics days, through parliamentary staff roles to preselection and parliament, and often from law and accounting; politics becomes an elite career path rather than a vehicle of public service, and the public seems either unaware of that reality, or powerless to influence its reformation.

> But although voters remain engaged with political issues that are important to them, they have lost their connection with the central operating agents of democratic politics in the West – political parties (*Our Very Own Brexit*, p. 28).

Both parties are so disengaged from their imagined constituents that they have been making decisions based on a depleted membership base, with the desires and interests of whom they are increasingly out of touch. The LNP have made policy they think is supportive of the business sector generally, and some of the business sector is saying 'we don't want that'. In 2019, Labor lost the unlosable election on a bold platform of actual reform they believed to be in the interest of their faithful and for the benefit of the majority. Although the platform contained much that was in the public interest, it wasn't received as such, wasn't effectively communicated, and Labor was humiliated!

Having lost their traditional 'faithful', and having not adequately drawn from those in that group with skill and experience, both parties have resorted to 'professional' political representatives who seem to exist in a vacuum of their own making, with little real reference to those they purport to represent. Both parties seem to be wandering in a wilderness of their own incompetence, and have created the great disconnect between politics and the society for whom it is supposed to exist. Neither party seems to exist for the good of the public.

The public disengagement from the major parties – due to political 'interests' that are not those of the voters – is reflected in the rise of 'Independent' Political Representatives and minor parties, heralding the declining relevance of the major parties. Qualified commentators like Sam Roggeveen tell us that the trend could see us with minority governments for the foreseeable future – an outcome not inconsistent with reasonable government as indicated by much of the present European political landscape.

Having lost contact with their public base, having professionalised and lost sight of why they are in parliament, each of the major parties has degenerated into an ideological culture war both with their opposition, and with members of their own party. Existential panic and its associated wrangling adversarialism is the result; ill-conceived ideology has replaced public service as the focus, and the self-distancing public is far more aware of that reality than the politicians! But, more than the mere shift from *legitimacy* to *professionalism* in politicians, the party system has far deeper flaws, and democracy cannot exist in practice unless those flaws are recognised and transformed.

The *party system* is the problem. We need to hear that and take it on board: the *party system* is the problem. And that system is broken beyond repair! It never was one that would last from birth to old age of any society. It worked – sort of – for early years. But it's now well past its use-by date. Not only is the system broken, the parties themselves are broken. The very names *Liberal* and *Labor* are no longer accurate labels. The Liberal Coalition has devolved to vapid conservatism; little more than upholding social institutions based on the British cultural tradition of class distinction and rule by the privileged, titled and *landed gentry*. Their goal is to conserve the rights and privilege of the elite and wealthy of society, and resist any change that might threaten that privilege.

True Liberalism in politics is a moral philosophy upholding liberty, justice and equality for all citizens. The LNP has shifted quite far from that position. A more accurate description of that party could be the 'NLNP' – the Neo-Liberal National Party for, as with Neo-Classical Economics, in its *newness* its fundamental essence is deformed and impotent.

Labor, too, has moved so far to the right, that it raced past most of its former liberalism – its championing a 'fair-go' for the general citizenry – for fear of being seen by the electorate as 'leftist' which, by the lies and manipulation of the conservatives, has come to be thought of as something evil, totalitarian and to be avoided! The terms Socialism and Communism are thrown about mischievously to deflect public attention away from the totalitarianism of capitalism. More on that later. At present there is no party serving the general population. And, for reasons I hope to clarify here, no *party* will ever be able to.

Winston Churchill is famously quoted as saying *'democracy is the worst form of government – except for all the others.'* But just because democracy is the least-worst form of government doesn't mean it shouldn't be modified significantly to actually make it democratic.

Democracy meaning *rule by the people* is sometimes thought of as *the rule of the mediocre*. Albert Einstein added to that sentiment. He is reported to have said '*the majority of the stupid is invincible and guaranteed for all time. The terror of their tyranny, however, is alleviated by their lack of consistency*'. More on that in a later section. First, let's consider further what makes the party system a 'failure'.

The party is necessarily and incontrovertibly adversarial because it comprises individuals each with a unique conscience, beliefs, values and motivations. The adversarial nature of the party system is wasteful in the extreme. It wastes valuable human energy that could be put to creative, productive activity. It wastes enormous resources of public dollars paying over-generous salaries and conditions for party-politicians who, despite their best intentions, because of the party machinery don't seem to achieve much of value for their constituents or for the nation. But of grave importance and eternal significance, the party system is wasteful of 'life'. Why do I say that? Simply because *the party system denies the attainment of justice and truth.* And why do I say that? Because a party doesn't have a conscience! Individual members each have a conscience! Each individual has beliefs, values, desires and motivations. But, when they join a party, their beliefs, values, desires and motivations – their consciences – are no longer allowed voice as the party has a *line* it follows; an agenda; a *platform*; a commitment to serve certain interest groups. The individual is no longer an individual; they are required to be loyal to the mind of the party, whether they agree with the party line or not. Their conscience is denied expression. There are rare occasions when the party allows a *conscience vote*. What an absurd situation! Conscience is allowed only occasionally! One would think that every personal conscience should be operating front and centre on every issue in order for wisdom/truth to be discerned and, thus, justice to be enacted.

The matter of 'will'

Jean-Jacques Rousseau's profound contribution to political philosophy is that he identified and exposed the interplay of what he called the *will of all* or *particular will* (each person's self-interested will) and the *general will* (the discerned will of the *sovereign* – the community; the public good). Herein lies the great challenge for us: to engage each member of the community as legitimate, contributing citizens, educating ourselves to comprehend what is required to be a unified community/nation; to find a way for each *particular will* to be expressed and engaged in an honouring-search for a *general will* that best addresses the public good (*'The Social Contract'*). Many politicians and members of political parties seem either not to have any awareness of, or respect of and fidelity to, the philosophy governing functional social arrangements. The primary focus is on the *particular will* or self-interest.

Parties and their representatives and members are governed by – controlled by – self-interest. The *general will* – what is right, true, good for all members of the public (Rousseau's *'sovereign'*) – doesn't get a look in; the voices of privilege, wealth and power – or perhaps charisma and emotional manipulation of salesmanship – are able to influence policy to serve their self-interest and ensure their benefits.

How, then, is the party democratic? How is it facilitating the common good – the *general will* – if the common views of all its members are being denied in favour of an arbitrary position driven by minority power and interest groups? It is difficult to see how a party could be democratic! Whatever the party may earnestly desire, think or say about its operation, because of the forces that drive it, it is not able to – or willing to – pursue truth and the public good. It is only interested in staying in what it calls 'power'; only interested in remaining in favour with those interest groups that will sustain it and ensure its tenure. Those interest groups also seem to ensure privileged 'post-political life' for many politicians. The party – be it political, religious, economic or any other variety – is, therefore, unable to bring about justice; is unable to serve truth; unable to access wisdom; unable to seek and act for the public good.

Can we not say, then, that as the party system is unable to produce good, it necessarily produces evil? '*A good tree cannot produce bad fruit, neither can a corrupt tree produce good fruit* (*Luke* 6:43-45). Farmers and gardeners cut down and burn badly-diseased trees. The party is a badly-diseased tree and, therefore, should it not be destroyed? This is not my idea or a new idea; I am merely a reminder that wise women and men throughout history have railed against dysfunctional and destructive party systems. But, because of the power of vested interests in maintaining the status-quo – because of the enormous amounts of money and energy poured into hiding the awful truth about the flawed system – the dysfunction has not been successfully challenged and healed. In the 1940s, brilliant philosopher, university teacher, Christian mystic theologian, activist, and acclaimed author, Simone Weil, made what was then, is now and (unless we wake up, listen and change) always will be, an outlandish statement. In fact, she made many such statements. Today, she'd make the grade as a *whistle-blower*; one of the wise and courageous ones speaking out against an obvious evil. And the powers-that-be attempted to discredit her any way they could, as they are today with those speaking for justice, for freedom of journalism and the public's right to know.

That's the nature of philosophical, spiritual, human wisdom; it seems outlandish to the average, comfortable, lazy mind. But when one is seeing with more than a superficial glance at life, the outlandishness dissolves. But to return to the statement we want to discuss here, Simone Weil wrote a small book advocating *The Complete Abolition of All Political Parties*, (1957, translated by Simon Leys, 2013, New York Review publishers). Central to the reasons for such advocacy was her indisputable assertion mentioned above that membership of a political party effectively eliminated the possibility of truth, justice and the public good.

How so? She explains.

The 'first quality of a politician is integrity. Integrity requires independence of judgment. Independence of judgment rejects partisan edicts because partisan edicts stifle a person's conscience, all sense of justice, and the very taste of truth' (Quote from translator's foreword).

The quote continues, 'without such truths, parliament is a circus provoking dismay and contempt in the public'.

Dismay and contempt for parliament is alive and well in our world today almost anywhere we care to look.

Common sense may tell us that the only legitimate reason for preserving anything is its 'goodness' – that which Weil suggests can be qualified as *'truth, justice and the public good'* (*The Complete Abolition*, p. 4), i.e. that which is humanly beneficial and life-giving for the majority of the public; that which all need for a life of dignity, equity and security. Weil states bluntly that parties are 'evil', that the evil is evident, and she asks these questions (p. 4): *'Is there enough good to compensate for their evils and make their preservation desirable?* (If they are evil they can only produce more evil as *'evil begets evil and good begets good'*. *'A good tree cannot bear bad fruit; a rotten tree never bears good fruit.'*) *'Do they do the slightest bit of good?* How do we define 'good'? Good for whom? Good from whose perspective? A famous parable from G. K. Chesterton may illustrate the point.

> Suppose that a great commotion arises in the street about something, let us say a lamp post, which many influential persons seek to pull down. A grey-clad monk, who is in the spirit of the middle ages, is approached upon the matter and begins to say, in the arid manner of the Schoolmen, 'Let us first of all consider, my brethren, the value of Light. If Light be itself good...'. At this point, he is somewhat excusably knocked down. All the people make a rush for the lamp post, the lamp post is down in ten minutes, and they go about congratulating each other on their mediaeval practicality. But as things go on, they do not work out so easily. Some people have pulled the lamp post down because they wanted the electric light; some because they wanted old iron; some because they wanted darkness, because their deeds were evil. Some thought it not enough of a lamp post, some too much;

some acted because they wanted to smash municipal machinery; some because they wanted to smash anything. And there is war in the night, no man knowing whom he strikes. So, gradually and inevitably, today, tomorrow or the next day, there comes back the conviction that the monk was right after all, and that all depends on what is the philosophy of Light. Only what we might have discussed under the gas-lamp, we now must discuss in the dark.

(G. K, Chesterton, *Heretics*, 1905)

Interest groups – *parties* – can only ever act in their own interests – or the interests of those whom they serve. They are not able to think and act beyond themselves – beyond their *particular wills*; they are not able to search for and act towards the *general will* – the public good for the sustainable wellbeing of the entire nation including, obviously, the physical environment that sustains all life.

The 'Good' in Democracy?

In this world, very little – if anything – is either totally good or totally bad. If we see correctly, if we see with open minds, hearts and engaged spirits, we can find both good and bad, positive and negative, in almost every experience of life. And, certainly, within our very selves, if we are honest and courageous. Democracy is no exception. It offers a great many benefits, freedoms, opportunities and possibilities that most other systems of political and social organisation do not, although other systems, too, are not without valuable aspects.

Unfortunately, democracy has become conflated and identified with the system of the *party*; we have accepted the conditioning – the lie – that democracy means the (Westminster) 'party system'. The earliest beginnings of democracy did not include membership of, and allegiance to, a party. Notwithstanding, Weil argues that democracy or majority rule is not good in itself; it is merely a means *towards* goodness. Democratic, legal processes don't guarantee goodness. Partisan lobbyists and pressure interests (mis)lead parliament to produce public policy which doesn't result in goodness for all.

Weil reminds us that crime and mendacity are never legitimate (*The Complete Abolition*, p. 21.). Laws are traditionally made by rich, powerful people and for their own economic benefit and that of their friends and associates. Because something is legal doesn't make it just or true. A leader promising to uphold the law is not necessarily supporting anything good or democratic. That a corporation can successfully sue a government for loss of revenue because of a law supporting the public good, indicates that something is radically wrong with our system.

In *The Social Contract*, Rousseau suggests that two keys in this discussion are *reason* and *passion*. He tells us that reason involves *conscience* and is individual; *passion* tends to and promotes collective group-think. Party politics is collective. The individual is subordinated to the collective. A nation influenced by collective passion, whipped up by lies, manipulation and vilification of others, becomes unanimous in crime. So, democracy ruled by party politics is complicit in all manner of unjust behaviour in the name of the *law*. Because all parties are necessarily caught up in the collective passion – the individual voices of reason and conscience being silenced – the 'circus' becomes passion against passion. And passions don't neutralise one another. They *'escalate and drown out the voices of truth and justice'* (*The Social Contract*, p. 8) The point to be made is that when passions are high - in the circumstances such as those we see in our parliamentary debates – *'it is likely that the individual voice is closer to truth than the collective'* (ibid. P. 9).

We don't really have democracy in Australia – certainly not true and effective democracy – because the opposing collective passions of the two major parties prevent members from expressing their personal views on the issues of public life. Further, members are prevented from seeking and considering what the *general will* might be. They are stuck between two options: their individual *particular will* and the *particular will of the party*. The *will* of the party does not produce democracy. And Einstein's unfortunate *invincible stupidity* of the masses seems to be self-perpetuating through abrogation of personal responsibility to become aware, informed and active in the process of 'government by the people'. Of course, the public is generally only aware of what they have been fed by government, media and hearsay; the average mind has been captured by propaganda of one kind or another. Too many of us don't think very deeply; too many of us belong to the 'lazy lot'!

For several generations in Australia, life has been too easy for many of us. Unfortunately, that ease is being rapidly eroded for an increasing number. Misguided loyalty to various belief systems – those of our parents, religions, education, social mores, etc. – has made us careless in how we approach our lives. But, even for the growing number who do think and speak out, the system seems to quarantine politicians from taking any notice of dissent. There seems to be no effective way to require politicians to consider and heed the raised voices of justice and truth. At the time of writing, there is even one senior government minister who is refusing to comply with a court directive to release a woman who has been languishing in detention for eight years! If our judiciary is no longer independent and able to direct justice, we are in deep trouble.

In the Eastern Europe of history, and in some parts today, totalitarianism has worked its evil with the minds of millions of citizens. Writing about this phenomenon, Czeslaw Milosz in his 1951 classic, *The Captive Mind*, says:

> Everything, thus, takes us back to the mastery of the mind. People who attend a 'club' submit to a collective rhythm, and so come to feel that it is absurd to think differently from the collective. The collective is composed of units of doubt; but as these individuals pronounce the ritual phrases and sing the ritual songs, they create a collective aura to which they in turn surrender. Despite its apparent appeal to reason, the club's activity comes under the heading of collective magic. The rationalism of the doctrine is fused with sorcery, and the two strengthen each other. Free discussion is, of course, eliminated.

(*The Captive Mind*, Penguin Classic, 2001, p. 199).

Here in Australia at present, it's not much of a stretch to use the description 'totalitarianism' for our government. Although we still have great freedoms of speech and action – at least in theory – at the time of writing, those democratic freedoms – to speak, protest and demonstrate against specific government agendas – are being systematically eroded by a government desperately out of step with an increasing majority of citizens. Laws are being framed to criminalise lobbying and demonstrating for action on climate change, for example, which has become the current, primary concern for the majority of citizens. This is a government – and system – in steep decline, as fear has taken over as the main motivator – the main tool – to achieve control. Milosz reminds us that 'when people are divided into "loyalists" and "criminals", a premium is placed on every type of conformist, coward and hireling, whereas among the "criminals", one finds a significant high percentage of people who are direct, sincere, and true to themselves. From the social point of view, these persons would constitute the best guarantee that the future development of the social organism would be towards good' (*The Captive Mind*).

The Political 'Game'

Weil notes that party politics has its origins in aristocratic indulgence. The privilege of the rich and powerful allowed themselves to assume superior rights to *play* with the nation's people and assets. Parliament became a *game* that persists today, a fact that many politicians publicly and with levity acknowledge; an attitude that is an obscenity to a great many citizens, and ought to be to all. Whereas non-aristocratic beginnings of any public endeavour are generally flavoured by seriousness. Governance of a nation ought to be treated with seriousness. People's lives and resources have become the *gambling chips*. Those lives and resources are not the property of the politicians, although too many party-politicians seems to think and act as if they are.

Political 'Qualities'

As mentioned earlier, Rousseau goes on to say this about his two premises: first, *reason* perceives and chooses what is just and innocently useful (whereas much crime is motivated by passion). Secondly, reason is identical in all people whereas their passions most often differ. If we collect all individual thoughts/opinion and compare them, they are likely to coincide inasmuch as they are reasonable and just, whereas they will differ inasmuch as they are unjust or mistaken. *Truth is 'One'. Justice is 'One'.* (Rousseau in Weil, *The Complete Abolition of all Political Parties*, p. 6).

Again, according to Rousseau, there is an infinite variety of injustices. Men and women converge on what is just and true, whereas mendacity and crime make them diverge without end. The unjust will of a nation is by no means superior to the unjust will of a single individual. He states that there are two conditions required in a nation for the general will to be applied.

1. There must be no form of collective passion influencing the individual intent and expression (no propaganda / pressure / passion / conditioning.)
2. People should express their will regarding the problems of public life – not merely choosing among individuals or groups.

Considering that, let's look at what political parties are according to the criteria of truth, justice and the public interest. According to Weil, there are three main characteristics of political parties; characteristics that simple observation will verify.

1. A machine to generate collective passion.
2. An organisation designed to exert collective pressure on the minds of all its individual members.
3. Its first objective and ultimate goal is its own growth without limit (Weil, p. 11.).

Parties need to secure vast amounts of power – members, money, supporters, donors – and no amount is ever deemed enough. Growth is the mantra. But the absence of *individual thought* creates a sense of permanent impotence. The party spruiks 'public interest', 'national interest' but, in reality, the party having and remaining in power *is* the interest.

The party becomes its own end and, therefore according to Weil, is idolatrous and evil.

The collective psyche of the party's function operates to make goals vague. If goals were real and based in truth and justice, they would be pursued with *grave attention and effort*. Weil makes the point that we can't serve God and mammon; we can't serve truth and self-interest. As truth is lost in the party machinations of self-interest and serving partisan interests, goodness itself is lost and, with it, the very idea of what is actually 'good'.

In the party system, growth has become *goodness*. (And infinite growth in a finite system is supposed to be intelligent and believable!) The party exerts collective pressure on the minds of the public to believe their story. The pressure is real, targeted, sustained, professionally proclaimed and, repeated often enough, lies become truth. And instead of the public being horrified, we accept it as 'the way life is'.

Growing numbers of concerned citizens throughout the world are saying, 'NO'; that's not the way it is!

But it is the way life has become because we abrogate responsibility for thinking and researching for ourselves, mindlessly accepting misinformation and outright lies we are fed by the parties. Parties don't educate the public; they condition, propagandise and control. They punish the recalcitrant, expel, vilify, etc. anyone who doesn't 'toe the party line'. And they do the same to any opposition party or independent representative. Parties are petrified of losing 'power', and turn themselves inside out to discredit any opposition to their particular ideology.

Weil and Rousseau tell us that the party will not allow any member to hold views that are contrary to the collective passion of the party. From time-to-time, members do express contrary views and, when they do, the party distances itself from those expressions. Sounding magnanimous, they may say they accept that members have the right to express personal views, but reaffirm *they are not the views of the party*. Those members are usually censured or punished in some way by the party. 'Faithful' members who over-identify with party position, unwittingly or otherwise, give up any intention towards truth, justice and the public good, which are, thus, sacrificed on the altar of ideology.

It is impossible to seek and attend to truth, justice and the public interest and at the same time maintain an attitude that is expected of members of a political party.'... 'Political parties are mechanisms that ensure not a single mind can attend to the effect of perceiving what is good, just and true'... That being the case, 'nothing is decided, nothing is executed except measures that run contrary to the public interest, to justice and truth. (Weil, p. 24)

The ones served are only the minority partisan interests who financially and doctrinally underwrite, engineer and sustain the party ideology. Why would a person, corporation or group financially support a certain party if not to expect and reap some benefit? Weil, who sees deeply and profoundly into the machinations of the political party, further says *'if we were to trust the organisation of public life to the devil, he could not invent a more clever device'* (p. 24). Challenging words! Seeing the truth of the spiritual reality underpinning life, she grieves that our *'inner light is discarded instead of it guiding the spiritual destiny of human creatures.'* (ibid).

For us to achieve democracy, our challenge, according to Weil – and there seems to be no rational argument that will refute her on this – is to find a process that solves two problems:

1. How to give men and women who form the nation 'the opportunity to express, from time to time, their judgment on the main problems of public life'.
2. How, when questions are being put to the people, can one prevent their being infected by collective passion? (Weil, p. 10).

70

It is clear that, in living memory, the governance practices of the vast majority of nations haven't ever come close to being truly democratic. Truth and justice and then the public good have been, and are being, drowned out by the noise of collective passion and the interests that drive those passions. No *party* facilitates or permits these two conditions being met. The party refuses to put truth and justice at the top of their agenda.

It is a tragic irony that those who relinquish truth and justice don't suffer, whereas the party punishes those who are insubordinate to the parties of *no truth and justice*. The party even punishes and vilifies outsiders who expose political misbehaviour. The insulting term 'whistle-blower' is ascribed to those who are actually 'truth-tellers'. Is it any wonder that the world is in such a mess! Weil urges us to *'strenuously protect our inner faculties of judgment against the turmoil of personal hopes and fears that are influenced by the collective passion of the party'*, and exhorts us to *'run from anyone who wields the whip'* (Weil, p. 23). 'Faithful' members, their 'inner light' thus darkened, are forced to 'lie'. Let's talk about that statement.

The 'Lie Trap'

To belong to a party, one must subscribe to and abide by the ideology, rules, practices etc. of that party. So, a member effectively renounces their individual beliefs, conscience, thoughts and feelings about matters being considered by the party. It is perhaps useful to reflect on the fact that there is no such thing as a *party opinion*. The party is a group made up of individuals all of whom have unique, individual, personal thoughts, feelings, beliefs and opinions. So, for the party to choose and hold to a position on any matter, the individuals' positions are subordinated if not denied completely. All individual 'truths' – all *particular wills* – are neutralised by the party's 'truth' – the party's *particular will*. Remember, neither makes the grade as the *general will* about which we spoke earlier; that *will*, the aim of which is the common good. No party is capable of achieving the *general will* which is grounded in truth and justice, i.e. the absence of lies, deceptions, conditioning, the interests and passions of the collective, lobbying, etc.

The party member is, thus, in a position in which they have no option but to *lie*.

According to Weil, a party member cannot NOT lie! A *democratic* party member! Democratic? Seriously? Weil goes on to suggest there are three types of lies.

Lies to the party (about what one really believes).

Lies to the public (expressing the party line rather than what they personally believe).

Lies to themselves (convincing themselves that the party line is acceptable).

Weil suggests that the first lie is the least serious as it is a lie to an organisational structure which is bound by interests that serve a partisan group rather than the overall public good.

The second lie is more serious. It deceives the public who *deserve* truth but who are being violated because they are not getting truth. This brand of lie probably goes some way to explain why party politicians rarely provide a direct, unequivocal answer. They are conflicted within themselves and are unable or unwilling to speak truthfully.

The third lie – the lie to themselves – is arguably the most dangerous as, according to Weil, it effectively *darkens the inner light*. The party politician has silenced his or her conscience, violated his or her soul, and no longer has access to truth. This type of lie is the most pervasive and destructive, thus, the most tragic for the individual and for the society that looks to them for wise guidance.

Summarising the value of political parties, Weil sees them as bad in principle and practice, bad in impact, wasteful, adversarial, corrupted by adherence to mendacity, unable to carry out public functions, unjust, opaque, vague, impotent. She notes that measures that present no inconvenience are least likely to be adopted by parties whose thinking is if it's so simple, why wasn't it done years ago? Common sense might say, 'why indeed wasn't it done? It is often demonstrated that great things are simple. Our political party system is shackled by 'for and against' versus 'all things well thought through, uniquely expressed and held together as parts of the whole'. Weil makes the point that *'for and against'* is *intellectual laziness – leprosy'* (ibid. p. 34.).

Weil's overall view is that *'every party is totalitarian potentially and by aspiration, and should therefore be abolished'* (ibid., p. 11). It is hard to argue against her simple, profound logic, yet the 'machine' does, and does so effectively. Look at the issue of climate change, for example. For several decades, the parties have effectively denounced the scientific experts and convinced the unthinking masses that climate change is a myth. With developing evidence and public resistance to their spin, recently they reluctantly conceded that climate change is a fact, but it isn't caused by human activity. At the time of writing, most in government are now conceding humans are *partly* responsible for climate change, but the government of the day – the LNP – remains vociferously adamant that they have no intention to change their policy on mitigation or CO2 targets. The partisans have yet to comprehensively accept that human activity has indeed been instrumental in climate change, and commit immediately to effective mitigation in the national and global public interest. There still isn't the personal or collective will to make these simple changes from a system that is manifestly dysfunctional.

Restoration

How can we restore the essential qualities of personal integrity, democracy and domestic security? For several hundred years, women and men of wisdom and vision have been trying to eliminate the flaws in our dysfunctional political and economic systems. Whilst it would be hopeful to think that an appropriate change may happen, the current signs are not yet promising.

Whilst it is unlikely that all political parties will be abolished any time soon – as necessary as that seems to be – it is clear that major reform to their constitution and function must be achieved. Successive governments talk about 'reform'. But that is just a word they spin; it has had little substance in action. The reality is that, because of their blind adherence to a system, the flaws which they are unable or unwilling to recognise because their thinking is inextricably shackled to a flawed paradigm, they have zero chance of achieving anything like 'reform'. Reform means growth for good – for the majority, not just a tax break for the few at the top, for example. Apart from a growing cohort of scientific experts and accurately-informed young people, functional action at government level is virtually non-existent in Australia and elsewhere. This growing group of informed, concerned citizens who are speaking out and demonstrating against the resistant administrations knows that the major actions needed to be taken include the following:

- Completely redesign politics to eliminate the present party dysfunction thus freeing all parliamentary rep- resentatives to follow their personal conscience on all matters, restoring integrity and the potential for democracy, and opening the way for truth, justice and the public good. Apart from on a village-community level, the world doesn't have such a model currently operating but, if we accepted the validity of, and operated out of, a *general will*, a model could be easily developed and simply implemented over a fairly short period of time. In indigenous societies, small communities, in philosophy and good religion, we have some clues.
- Foster and require *disinterest* in politics, i.e., *non-partisan interests*; vigorously and courageously pursue and promote only the public good; the *general will*; the *sovereign*. In today's world the public good is now global and includes matters that affect all life on earth; matters such

as deforestation, climate change, enmity, oppression, tribalising, borders, resource sharing. Avoid politics of 'what's in it for me'? How?

- Completely eliminate political donations by making political donations criminal acts, thereby removing the influence of interest groups. If democracy is 'sponsored', it becomes a system of government 'of the people, by the people and for *only some* of the people'; those who sponsor it. If democracy is sponsored, it is reduced to being merely a system for electing political representatives, and will fail to deliver outcomes of justice and equity for all citizens. We humans have personal agendas; we generally want life to be the way we want it. Those who donate to a political representative or party are no different. They generally expect something for their donations. The 'public good' of Weil and others can be taken to mean justice and care for the earth and all its life forms. When political and economic decisions can be influenced by partisan interests, democracy is unable to deliver its potential for good. Pro-rata funds could and should be provided from the public purse.
- Make political lobbying illegal for anything other than the public good; for what Rousseau calls 'the *general will*'.
- Pursue policies of mature humanity; friendship and inclusion and defocus policies of fear, aggression and self-interest. Policies such as the euphemistically-labelled 'free trade' agreements which generally benefit only a sector of any nation.
- Commit to immediate, radical action to transition to renewable energy to secure a zero-emission economy and, at the same time, dramatically-reduce costs for

households and industry, agriculture, transport. Modelling on abundant, available resources in Australia demonstrates that we could easily become a zero-emission nation by 2030. (See Ross Garnaut's 2019 book, *Super-Power*) Renewable energy could see us becoming a globally-competitive industrial nation providing goods and materials to the world manufactured here from our vast mineral resources. Ross Garnaut states that, using renewable energies, '*Converting one quarter of Australian iron oxide and one half of aluminium oxide exports to metal would add more value and jobs than current coal and gas combined*'. (*Super-Power*, p. 185). Renewable energy could economically-produce hydrogen for domestic fuel and export, and ammonia as a carrier of hydrogen to export renewable energy. The widespread availability of renewable energy, together with appropriate national transmission infrastructure, would see decentralisation of industries and communities throughout the nation, reducing the pressures of congestion in and around major cities, and radically-increasing quality of life and employment opportunities.

- Eliminate the abject waste of the adversarialism of *government* and *opposition* by eliminating parties. To possess the required integrity demanded of their responsibilities, all political representatives need to be in the business of seeking the common good; the public good. A new social arrangement for a just, civil society needs to be devised.

- Prioritise domestic economy, domestic security, Australian-owned small, medium and large industry and sustainable and equitable social life for all citizens. International trade – though both unavoidable and desirable in our globalised world – should be secondary. Minimise dependence on uncontrollable international supply of essential materials and goods. International relations – because we are a global community now – need to be ascribed the same human morality as that of domestic relations.

- Realise that the primary responsibility of government is to ensure the welfare of all citizens: ensure 'functional finance' in a 'controlled and balanced economy', to avoid unemployment, control inflation and ensure equitable distribution of wealth by eliminating monopolistic owner-ship and control of public resources. By means of a Federal 'job guarantee', ensure that every citizen wanting to work has access to meaningful employment and adequate remuneration to provide livelihoods of sufficiency and dignity, whilst creating an effective provision of essential infrastructure and 'care' for all citizens composing Australian society. This measure could eliminate the indignity and waste of Centrelink queues, provide personal security and significance, elevate self-worth, return spending back into the economy, create a constantly-employable workforce, dramatically-reduce meaninglessness and associated substance abuse, depression, anxiety and despair, and generally maximise physical, emotional, mental and spiritual health.
- Develop mutually beneficial, secure and honouring relations with regional neighbours and trading partners, and reduce current trading dependencies.
- Transform education by teaching, at all levels, the reality of our complex, profound, spiritual and social humanity,

philosophical interconnectedness and oneness of all beings and of the material universe. Increase focus on the intra and inter realities of life rather than primarily on the outer illusion of the physical and material, and of wealth and power.

None of these requirements is easy because they require each of us to *return to the Centre* (see Bede Griffiths, *Return to the Center*, Templegate, 1982) of our being – to the life-giving spirit place within us in which Wisdom and Truth are to be found, and from which flows abundant life and all goodness.

First Nations Wisdom

As mentioned at the end of last chapter, there is a model of political, economic and societal organisation and management that has been operating sustainably in the Aboriginal culture for something like 60,000 years here in Australia. Unfortunately – as is the case for all peoples – the Europeans could only view life from the only model they knew and, naturally, thought to be the only one and the best one. We can't blame them for not knowing what they couldn't be expected to know *in the normal way of knowing*, i.e. with the intellect and in the light of their European socialisation. But, as we will discuss in the next chapters, the intellect alone is not adequately equipped to reveal wisdom, truth and, thus, a just way of being fully human.

The economic key to the Aboriginal model is that they had a profound connection to land – to creation; a connection that was inextricably interwoven with a deep spirituality and philosophy of belonging to and in creation; 'one' with it! They correctly understood that no *creature* can *own* creation but, rather, all creatures are owned by – belong to – creation. Of course, their humanity allowed disharmony to arise from time to time, although never degenerating into all-out violence and mutual destruction. Why? A major reason is that the *woman* – the presence of female nurture, gentleness and life-giving – enjoyed honour and influence with the man, the one more geared to physical force. The vital immanence of the *anima* ensured a reverence and, thus, care for creation that ensured the sustainability of both the family and the ecosphere. In less than only three centuries, our European model of *being* has wrought great destruction of that delicate ecosphere. How we can see our way as being superior defies all reason.

What about political organisation? How does our politics compare with that of the Aboriginal peoples? For a start, Aboriginal leaders were Elders – not only in age, because, as Bruce Pascoe, explains in *Dark Emu*,

> ... not all who became old were included in the final decision-making process; that authority was received following the complex trials of initiation. To that extent, Elders became the equivalent of senior clergy, judges, and politicians. Their role was codified by levels of initiation that elevated them to a position where they could influence particular areas of policy. Their election to that position was gradual and complex, usually through the initiation process, but they didn't assume that position by force or inheritance. They earned the respect of their fellows.
>
> All other processes of delivering justice, protecting the peace, managing hierarchy and social roles as well as the

dividing up of the land's wealth were defined by ancestral law, and interpreted by those chosen as senior Elders. Of all the systems humans have devised to manage their lives on earth, Aboriginal government looks most like the democratic model.

(Bruce Pascoe, *Dark Emu*, Magabala Books, Western Australia, 2014)

The 'Oldest Socialism'

The shining success of the Aboriginal model is due to the fact that it is truly Socialist! But before anyone gets too excited by that term, a brief note of what Socialism *is* and *is not* is necessary. Simply, in its truest expression, Socialism deals with the socialisation of a civil, equitable society supported by wise and just economic and political arrangements, and the inculcation of *social imposition from within the person and community*.

Socialism, as it has historically been experienced, was corrupted by *coercive force* of either state, church, trades unions or other systematic *impositions from outside the person and community*. It seems clear that, if we are to have a future of fairness for all and sustainability of the earth's ecosphere and finite resources, that future is dependent on turning away from the failures of historic Communism, Socialism and Capitalism, and turning towards a version of Socialism expressed in historic Aboriginal society. It is instructive to note that the historic Jesus Christ advocated for such a society, and provided the guidance and personal inner resources for us to bring it to fruition. The provision is *acquired* and *infused* mystical knowledge.

Aboriginal Elders were governed by physical and spiritual wisdom; *acquired* and *infused* knowledge of all aspects of the lives of their people, other creatures and the land itself. *Acquired* by observing the country and the seasons, and through learning from their elders and people, and in the normal ways of learning and knowing. *Infused* because, through spiritual communication with their universe, they came to know truths that many non-indigenous people are yet to learn; that we seem unable or unwilling to learn. The most glaring example at present is the wholesale destruction of the environment and the connection of European activity to climate change and its impact on extreme, devastating weather events.

How are our political 'elders' (notice the lower case 'e') selected? Are they old? Not necessarily. Are they experienced in the matters they oversee? Not necessarily. (Many of them are academic lawyers, accountants, business people, partisan-interested people, political staffers who drifted up in rank and influence – none of which *necessarily* disqualifies them, of course). Are they wise in the ways of environmental care? Not necessarily. Are their values consistent with equitable distribution of the land's wealth? In many cases, no! Do they see humans as being part of creation? It seems some do not! Do they operate with a deep spiritual understanding of the interconnectedness of the earth's eco-systems? No! Do they care for life more than material wealth? It often seems not! Do they operate as if there are classes of human beings? Sadly, some do! Do they think that land and its resources are to be privately owned for personal benefit? It would appear so!

We could go on, but it's a bit depressing! Neither an in-depth nor cursory analysis could cause us to arrive at any conclusion other than our way is radically inferior to that practised by our First Nation Elders and their peoples on many matters. Is there a solution to our decline? Happily, yes! But will we consider implementing it? Unless each of us is truthfully informed, courageously-engaged and soul-fully versed and focused, probably not! Our track record over the last 250 years isn't all that bright. But let's give ourselves the benefit of the doubt, and consider, in the next chapter, how we might reverse the decline on which we find ourselves.

Chapter 3
Unfair Social Organisation

Our unwitting or deliberate accession to, and embrace of, the flawed systems of politics and economics discussed above have caused the human community to devolve disturbingly. That devolution has had, and continues to have, a devastating impact on the fragile and intricately-balanced eco-systems of this beautiful, precious, God-given earth home. As we human beings are inextricably one with those eco-systems, we, too, are impacted. How are we impacted? A look around at the world we have shaped should cause each of us to grieve for the loss of the innocence and balance of nature and, indeed, our own loss of innocence and balance as simple, profound, equal children of the earth. But we are more than *of the earth*; arguably more-importantly, we are also *of the Spirit* – that mysterious quality that, somewhere within ourselves, we sense is Reality but can't be defined. But it can be alluded to and engaged with. We do that when we see a new-born human or other creature, a magnificent sunset, the mystical stillness of the first rays of morning light, a wild ocean whipped by winds that are felt but not seen, clouds forming and dissolving, the sweet smell of a forest floor (if we can find a forest that's not burnt or drowned), the hum of bees working the garden flowers, birds going about their business of song and dance and much more; glorious 'created beauty' moving us emotionally and deeply in wonderful and mysterious ways. And that's only the external beauty!

Learning 'Presence'

That mysterious reality is to be *internally* experienced in meditation, contemplation or prayer, beyond 'knowing' in the usual mental way of knowing. And, in those moments of *being with* the *presence of what is*, we feel somehow more alive and at peace; somehow closer to the truth of life. We no longer feel that sense of *emptiness*, that *something is missing*. Are we talking about religion or philosophy here? Is this consideration of the existential aspects of our common humanity? And, what's the value in that anyway? The answers to those questions are 'yes, yes and yes', and that the value is inestimable! Why? Because those who have always controlled the world and its systems – those who hold the wealth, power and influence – are obviously attempting to function without reference to anything greater than the indispensable but limited human intellect and ego, and their failure is great. What makes me say that? The mess the world is in makes me say that! Let's look at what we've achieved with our flawed systems of economics, politics and, thus, social organisation.

In *The Corruption of Economics* (Shepheard-Walwyn Publishers, 1994)), Mason Gaffney summarised the 'achievement' of the Neo-Classical Economists in a chapter entitled *'The Bitter Harvest'*. His socio-metric statistics are about circumstances in the United States in the 1990's. Today, three American families together own wealth equivalent to the combined wealth of half the American population. Because of historical and demographic considerations, our socio-metric statistics here in Australia are somewhat different, but that's not really relevant as the trends are parallel. And, since he wrote, the metrics in the U.S. have, of course, changed – for the worse! But the trend has not. The trajectory of social, political and economic structures and management of the U.S. continues into negative territory. The trajectory of those factors in Australia is the same. We could detail endless statistics of the decline in both countries, but statistics are tedious and superfluous. All that is really needed is for us to look, listen, feel, touch, smell and think about what is happening within and around us.

The Decline

Ask the woman, man or youth in the street. Wages are declining in real terms, unemployment and underemployment are increasing, prison populations are increasing, poverty is deepening for an increasing number, dramatically – increasing wealth is concentrating in the hands of a diminishing few. Meaninglessness, depression and despair are driving more people to self-harming behaviours of substance abuse, crime and suicide.

Morality is in decline, and even so-called *democratic* governments are trending towards totalitarianism – 'big-stick' politics, secrecy, deception, nationalism, denying public the right to know. Funding for education and health has declined in real terms as what is rightfully public revenue from natural resources is increasingly privatised. The unwise and wasteful strategy of sprawling, speculative housing developments with their exorbitant energy, transport and service demands puts the benefits of public land resources in the pockets of developers to the detriment of householders and would-be householders – that is, if a house were affordable. We continue to privatise essential services, we encourage alien ownership of national assets, we impose ever-increasingly complex taxes to finance our nation (where, as irrefutably-argued by Henry George in 1879, a single tax on the value of land and its resources would do all that is needed), and we promote a financial system based on increasing consumption rather than conservation and wise use of all resources.

The most disturbing consumption and inadequate conservation is that of the physical environment itself. At the time of writing, seven million hectares of Australia have been destroyed by unprecedented, catastrophic bushfires, many lives have been lost, several thousand dwellings and associated structures have been destroyed together with livestock, the loss of billions of native animals, birds, insects and other creatures is inestimable. Equally disturbing is the complete inadequacy of political leaders' response to this unprecedented disaster. Many political leaders are in denial that this is a climate emergency, and there is deafening silence from them in terms of action and policy reassessment.

Our expert fire chiefs are saying that air-attack resources are minimal and inadequate to mitigate, steer or extinguish the fires in forests inaccessible by land vehicles. These same expert fire chiefs warned the government more than a year earlier that we were facing an unprecedented summer with inadequate preparation. Their expressed concerns were ignored – in major cases not even responded to. The country burned. What prevents fire is reducing temperature, managing fuel load, and water. Water in lakes and rivers, water in the soil, and water in vegetation that produces cooling of the atmosphere.

Australia is a dry land. Life-giving water is limited and precious. Over-generous water allocation to mining interests remains a travesty. Water trading between investors, who have no interest or business in the use of water, is obscene! And our policies allow it. Considering water as *capital* removes its availability to those who need it for sustaining agriculture and life in general. Inappropriate land use practices, including certain unsustainable farming activities and logging of forests remain unchecked, depleting soil and atmospheric moisture. Micro-climate change amalgamates with global climate change. If that's not enough, beggaring belief, both major political parties are openly committed to continuing exploitation and use of coal and other fossil-fuels for power generation and national income. Neither political party seems to understand that we are *part of nature*, not separate from it. Neither party seems to have any will to subordinate self-seeking ideology to courageous enactment of common sense.

In the presence of a current social and environmental disaster brought on by prolonged drought and resulting in unprecedented, cataclysmic bushfires, the government seems arrogantly clinging to 'business as usual' policies; policies that are central to the creation of current problems, and will ensure their continuation into the future unless there is an about-face. The wholesale destruction of Australia's environment – and that of many other nations – remains the greatest moral failure of human history, and the single highest priority to be urgently reversed everywhere in the world.

Having said all that, Australia is still one of the very best countries in which to live. Australia is rich in every measure: its First Nations' peoples, inhabitants of this land for around 60,000 years; the hundreds of nationalities and cultures that have arrived in the last few hundred years; the magnificent, ancient wilderness from desert to mountain to coastline; the abundant mineral and earth resources; the wide range of climatic conditions. But some of the most important of those resources – the peoples, the cultures, the physical environment – are being subordinated to focus on production of wealth that finds its way inexorably into the possession of the already-wealthy and influential. The riches that, as Henry George stated, are *given by God for the benefit of all* are being legally but immorally allocated to the wealthy for their personal benefit. And they consider this arrangement a *democracy*. And we, the unthinking, lazy majority, accept that unfairness as 'that's just the way it is'.

And it is at present! But it doesn't have to be. As we have discussed above, there is a better arrangement, and we need to urgently develop it in order to sustain the life of the earth and all its creatures – including us.

The way of the Neo-Classical Economists in our world, and the capitalists whose bidding they do, is seeing millions on the move, displaced by the stupidity of endless wars driven by fear-based, mindless ideologies, greed for property, wealth and power. Millions are stateless and homeless. Women and children are sickeningly over-represented in the dispossession and despair. The climate has changed and continues to change due, in significant part, to human destruction of natural vegetation, dramatic increase in atmospheric carbon causing oceans to heat up and acidify, and the attitudes of the likes of J. B. Clarke (quoted in *The Corruption of Economics*, p. 100) who promoted 'speculation' as *'service to the community'*.

One might wonder to which community he was referring, and it certainly wasn't the general public. The environment continues to be trashed by greed or poverty-driven persons and communities, and governments either disempowered by the *interests* they serve, or unaware of the impact they are allowing. If it weren't for the *greed-driven* there wouldn't be the *poverty-driven*, for the latter is directly caused by the former. If awareness and value of our common humanity were widespread, neither would exist. Prison would reduce; optimism would become the norm; health issues such as obesity, lethargy, depression would decrease. Hope would replace despair. Faith would replace doubt. Meaningfulness would replace meaninglessness. No-one would have too much and no- one would have too little of the necessities for a life of dignity. Not utopia, but achievable if we were to return to our *Centre*. More on that in the next chapter.

Our nominal democracy is in disturbingly steep decline. Actually, it's never really made the grade as true democracy, as it was, and remains, based on the English system of privilege of the landed aristocracy. From the outset, the founding fathers (if mothers had been the 'founders', it may have turned out quite differently) devised the rules to secure privilege and ensure inequality. The culture of the time was that men are divided into those born to rule and control, and those born to be ruled and controlled. That obscenity arose from the minds of men rather than the Mind of Wisdom and Truth; the Mind of God being dismissed as somehow irrelevant or inferior to our post-modern, sophisticated, cleverness. Far from being a democracy, in reality what we have is closer to an oligarchy or plutocracy: the few who rule are the profit-takers. Henry George called them *rent-takers*; those who have appropriated the wealth but don't labour for it; those who ensure their personal benefit from public land resources, and direct the policies and practices of parliaments.

We are allowing, encouraging and rewarding monopolies to violate the individual. Slavery, although changed in appearance, is alive and (un)well. Slave labour producing commercial goods in American prisons, child slave labour in sweat-shops, backpacker and immigrant slave labour on farms and in factories, slavery of workers needing two and three jobs to make ends meet; slavery due to the fatally-flawed systems of economics and politics that divide one from another, and all from their Truest Self; their spirit; the *God-image* and deep central reality of each human being. And this 'great divide' is also from the earth that is our one and only home for the duration of our physical lives. Slavery to oppressive taxation, mortgage interest payments, production quotas and consumption, appearances, striving for status or wealth. Slavery where *freedom* was the design and remains the desire of all.

It all sounds a bit glum, doesn't it? And it is! And nothing is able to change for the better – nothing is able to achieve justice for the general public - unless and until, as we've said earlier, *land (including water and air)* is liberated from its conflation with *capital*, as per the thesis and paradigm of the visionary Henry George. Land and its resources must be recognised as belonging to all citizens. Land is not the product of labour or capital. As Henry George asserted, *'land is given by God for the benefit of all'*. George was merely reasserting the essence of the American Declaration of Independence in that *'all men are created equal; that they are endowed by their Creator with certain unalienable rights; that among these are life, liberty and the pursuit of happiness'*. We noted earlier that the original draft of that section was to be *'life, liberty and property'*. The surreptitious change to the wording of the Declaration meant that land would become personal property only of those who could afford to acquire it and lock it up for their personal benefit.

Because land has now been assimilated into 'capital', for conceptual purposes, nature is treated as just another marketable commodity. Its characteristics are assumed to be identical to those of an office building or a lathe. Thus, owners of urban land are free to exercise their monopoly power. Result: land speculation is the primary cause of the urban economy and the built environment. And yet, social scientists remain silent about this process, which to this day remains free to wreak havoc.

(Fred Harrison in *The Corruption of Economics*, p. 180.)

A Better Way

Henry George was not advocating any destructive, immediate reversal of land ownership. He was not about stripping anyone's wealth from them. He understood that any transition to a fairer system would require time, wisdom, and a new awareness of the need to gently and firmly replace *interest* with *disinterest*; replace *personal* interest with *public* interest. In Rousseau's terms, replace the *particular will* with the *general will*. Nevertheless, George was unequivocal that a just return to the public of the benefits of public land was essential for justice and truth and the public good; for the end to poverty, the redressing of inequity, and the creation of economic and political ethics and morality. For the return of meaning and motivation through access to opportunity and its associated reduction of criminal activity, the removal of the waste of speculative locking up land and resources that could be and should be earning *rent* for the public rather than the individual *developer/rent-taker*.

We, the public, have unwittingly allowed to come into existence laws that *socialise debt* and *privatise profit*. Taxpayers provide roads, energy and communication to new urban developments, and the developers and businesses enjoy the benefits. When, through negligence and incompetence, financial institutions get into trouble, the taxpayer bails them out. From time to time, labour-employing industries – many of which have significant foreign ownership – are also subsidised by the taxpayer; industries which make little contribution to public finance, and send vast profits overseas to their parent corporations. Of course, reversing the direction of profit-taking – *actual economic reform* – is a bit of an ask, isn't it? How can we expect the tiny minority to give up some of their wealth and privilege? How can we expect them to drop their perhaps generationally-held views of superiority of their personal human worth or self-assumed 'right to rule'? How can such attitudes be changed? History of philosophy and sensible religion – apart from practical mechanics – say there are two ways: *pushing* and *pulling*; *driving* and *drawing*.

Throughout the history of humankind, and increasingly in our world today, we are tending to *push and drive* rather than *pull and draw*. 'Big-stick' politics was mentioned earlier; nationalism and tribalism are the present, fear-based tendencies; totalitarian control of one flavour or another is today's leadership currency, and we looked at the results above. Pushing and driving is coercive, and no human being willingly chooses coercion; it doesn't work. Coercion generates resistance, resistance generates friction, friction generates heat and that heat cannot *not* be dissipated; it will be *expressed* either outwardly or inwardly. Both expressions are destructive of our common humanity. Of course, there will always be an indispensable need for laws and rules that push and drive to some extent because we human beings are wilful and don't always exercise our wills in the direction that is wise and good for us and all others. In Australia during the past few decades, the main political strategies have been lies, manipulation, fear-mongering, vilifying the alternative government and anyone who dares to speak against the capitalist agenda, and coercion; 'strong-man' politics.

Right now, we are experiencing an alarming rise in government efforts to disallow the public's right to know what's going on with the matters that affect all citizens. A journalist's mandate, human right and need to report truth, is being undermined by government's endeavours to enact draconian laws that are overtly anti-democratic. The government has assumed some kind of divine right to be secretive about its actions. They seem to have forgotten that government is owned by the people who entrusted to them the right to govern. There is steadily-growing public discontent with government failure to address issues that are of concern to the majority of citizens – in particular, the issue of climate change, the urgently-needed transition to renewable energy sources, and the humane treatment of the traumatised who exercise their human right to seek asylum.

The conservative government has been obsessed with producing a budget surplus they promised at the last election, as if that is of major significance to effectively administering governance over the range of social needs. The fact that they have been trashing essential public services to achieve their obsession seems to have escaped them – unless, as seems to be the case, they don't really care about the public.

Nobody apart from the government is remotely interested in a budget surplus! Furthermore, Modern Monetary Theory suggests that, within appropriate limits, deficits are normal, not 'bad', and actually required throughout a sovereign nation's cycles. A deficit actually boosts the economy by putting money into the pockets of all citizens via improved services and well-paying jobs. At the time of writing, a case in point is right now in Australia with the government forced by Covid-19 pandemic to abandon the quest for a surplus, and run up a significant deficit in order to mitigate the financial hardship caused by widespread losses of incomes to house-holders and businesses. A necessary and good deficit that, if expanded and extended, will enable a timely economic and social recovery.

But the government is so disengaged from the general voter – and even those they think they are representing – that their priorities remain theirs alone. Business, social and economic experts are saying that while money has never been cheaper government should be spending on infrastructure to stimulate the languishing economy and decrease pressures on households. Until the advent of Covid-19, the government had continued to run the agenda of those few corporatists whose bidding they do, continued to dismiss public sentiment and, worse, resorted to increasing force. This *pushing* – this *driving* – is the fear-reaction of a political party in decline and ignorance of the realities of functional finance. It is heartening to note that there is a steady trickle of competent people who are abandoning the conservative party in order to serve as independents. Moreover, it is heartening to note that we seem to be watching something of the collapse of the party system itself that has rarely been able to deliver what is needed for the common good.

The other way – *pulling* or *drawing* – is more esoteric, as it involves existential, religio- philosophic considerations that, for many in our increasingly-secular world, are not even on the personal or collective radar. We have been seduced into thinking that we're so clever now that we don't need anything more than our physical and mental capacities. That delusion – that acquired hubris - is a significant reason for our current difficulties. Wittingly or unwittingly, we have denied ourselves access to the very resource required for life in all its fullness to work. I refer to that mysterious, ineffable quality of *spirit* to which I gave considerable attention in my recent book, *Uncommon Sense: reclaiming humanity*. Sensible religion and classical philosophy affirm that Inner Reality, and assert the necessity of engaging with *spirit* in order for life to be manageable, meaningful, just and true. To that largely-absent yet vital consideration we will turn in the next chapter.

Chapter 4
A Better Way

lthough, as we've said above, *driving* is necessary in some measure – some rules are necessary, it is primarily *drawing* that will take us where we need to be. We need to give serious consideration to that One path to truth, justice and, thus, the public good; we need to realise that the path of Truth is a *non-rational* path. It is a Mysterious yet Real *spiritual* path; a path that the wisdom of historic mysticism calls 'non-attachment'; of surrender; of *'letting go of the need for life to be in a certain way for me to be happy'*. Wars, oppression, violence, injustice, each and every 'bad', are the result of holding onto shallow ideology of some description. My opinion. My idea. My truth. My money. My neighbourhood. My political party. My church, etc.; 'attachment' that sets one against another and results in destruction; alienation. Unless we renew our minds – unless we become aware that we are for the most part living *unconsciously attached to all manner of things* – we will continue to believe that *driving* is the only way to move forward. And move forward we will, but in a trajectory that is taking us *away from* who we are, and how we are to live that actually works! *Driving* without the wise guidance of *being drawn* by the reality of spirit – *the spirit* that is our *inner light* – will only ever continue to deepen the dysfunction we bring to ourselves, each other and to the life of the earth.

Departure and Return

A very long time ago, it seems that the human race *departed* from the Path that provided life. Various religions and philosophies have their specific ways of describing that *departure* – if, in fact, they even accept such an event has taken place. To observe the troubles in lives, communities, nations and the earth itself, it seems reasonable to conclude that we went wrong somewhere. The incessant disagreements, conflicts, wars, scrambling after more resources, wealth, power and control seem to indicate something radically wrong with the way we are approaching the human experience. What's wrong is indicated by the fact that almost every single human being desires to receive and give *love*, and yet much of our life-energy is spent on the exact opposite! How can that be?

Historic, 'mystical' Christianity, and other disciplines of mysticism, teach that we have departed from our deepest essential nature and, thus, optimum function as beings, and have attached to transient aspects of life in the physical world. We are *dualistic* in our thinking: right/wrong, good/bad, true/false, Labor/Conservative, my opinion/your opinion, etc, rather than *'what is the best outcome for the majority?'* We haven't been taught to engage in each present moment with our deepest Self – our Truest Nature – that which we might call 'heart/soul/spirit'; that depth or *fund* in us that enables us to hold contradictions and mystery with equanimity, and with no need to understand, control or resolve. Our dualistic thinking causes us to be more focussed on what was and what might be than what is. We 'misplace' our security in the physical realm that is temporary and cannot be held, and fail to place our security in the spiritual/transcendent realm in which, alone, peace and contentment are to be experienced.

Whether or not we believe in a spiritual entity – God of some imagining – most people have a belief that *'there is something out there'* (or *in here*) that they can't adequately describe or know in the usual way of 'knowing'. Most people sense that there is more to life 'than meets the eye' – a telling expression coming from beyond our consciousness when we consider the mysterious reality that can't be seen! What it is, how significant it is, and how we might engage with 'it' are the universal questions. And, given that we aren't doing too well with the 'knowing' we currently use, it would seem a good idea to investigate further what other resources we might bring to bear on this business called 'life'.

Now departure from any 'path' isn't necessarily a one-way journey. *Returns* are also eminently possible and, if the departure seems to be taking us nowhere good, then a *return* seems highly desirable and, arguably, essential. We find ourselves to have departed from what *works effectively for all life forms*. We find that we live in a world of increasing inequality, mistrust, wholesale-destruction, adversarialism, hopelessness, meaninglessness, fear. We are lost in the injustice of personal interest – the *particular will* of Rousseau; an ego manifestation. Fear and self-focus are in charge. Material wealth and the illusory 'power' it promises are in charge. Love and 'other' focuses are subordinated. The public good – Rousseau's *general will* – is increasingly a minor consideration if it is considered at all. It's clear we've departed from a workable path. It is clear we need a *return*.

Modern psychology, sensible religion and philosophy have been saying for some time that the *animus* – or masculine principle – has too much control and the *anima* – the feminine principle – too little. The Indian sage, Sadhguru, says *'whether you are a man or a woman, unless the feminine become alive in you, you will never experience the finer aspects of life'*. Thomas Merton, Richard Rohr, Joseph Campbell, Ekhart Tolle, Bernard of Clairvaux, Meister Eckhart, Teresa of Avila, Catherine of Siena, Jean Pierre de Causade, mystics throughout the ages have expressed similar views about the 'feminine principle' of 'whole-human being'. Our First Nations Peoples knew and lived something of that truth. Could we say the attached 'ego' has assumed control, and the 'non-dual' spirit has been usurped and subordinated'? Is an appropriate return hidden in such a proposition?

Resistance and Acceptance

We spoke above about *driving* or *drawing* and about what amounts to the ego's vehement resistance to being *driven or drawn*. The ego believes *it is* the driver. If we are correct in assuming that we are more than ego, if we accept that we are deeper than that and we could call that deeper aspect of ourselves transcendent *spirit*, and if we are prepared to submit to that possibility, we are then in a position to consider that we might be able to live with less *resistance*. In fact, we need to do more than consider, because the reality is that we are all going to die! Our physical lives, the duration of which we have no control, are going to end. So, basing our security on the physical would seem foolish in the extreme. If we can embrace that reality, if we can realise and wholeheartedly embrace our deepest 'non-physical' reality, there is nothing that is driving us anymore. There was no true security in that previous way of being, so there is nothing to lose that we weren't going to lose anyway, and there's 'life' to gain.

Jesus of Nazareth referred to this state as *eternal life*. There is now no fear. We can allow ourselves to be *drawn* by the gentle mystery of spirit which is for us. There is no need to resist that which is for us; that is on our side and that is concerned with our best interests. '*I have plans for your welfare, not for your destruction*', says the Lord, '*to give you a future and a hope*' (Jeremiah 29:11). If a departure occurred, it was from our *Truth – our Love Essence; our God –* that we departed and to which we need to return. We departed into ego and fear, resistance and violence. Our return is to spirit and love; embrace and peace; inclusion and simplicity; Oneness with all that is, right here and right now. There is no other place we can be, there is no other way that gives life to all of life.

As we look around us at our world of social organisation, we see the results of that well-meaning but inadequate ego and its *particular will*. We see that our attempts to organise, govern, lead, influence, produce and share mostly result in brokenness, inequality, injustice, untruth, partisanship, personal interest that denies *others* the rights we all take to be *our right*. Henry George spoke about the obscenity of abject poverty existing in the midst of great wealth; poverty created by an unjust system of access to, and distribution of, the necessities for a life of dignity for all; an unjust system created by men of little awareness of what it means to be fully human.

He spoke from his understanding and experience of, and belief in, the Way of the Historic and Cosmic Christ Spirit; the way of justice, mercy and compassion. Inherent in that 'way' is the opposition to oppression – of any kind – of one human being by another. George saw correctly that poverty arose from human-made laws that allowed resources *'given freely by God for the benefit of all'* to be held in private ownership and solely for the personal use of the 'owner'. He saw correctly that poverty was a spiritual issue. He saw correctly that poverty could not be eliminated unless those laws relating to private ownership were transformed to allow equitable provision for all, and care of the earth that sustains all life. Two essential changes are required: laws of humankind need to be based on justice and truth. And justice and truth are only revealed by willing acceptance of, and submission to, Universal Wisdom; the Law of 'God'; the law of Love. Such a submission engages us in an experience of our individual and, thus, corporate human *poverty*, a term that is generally thought of in the negative, but, in reality, is an increasingly rich and empowering positive. Let's try to explain.

In order to engage effectively with such a transformation, we need to clarify the definition of poverty, for poverty is not simply to do with material considerations. Although the term 'poverty' does mean, in the first instance, *material* poverty, it also has a discrete *spiritual* meaning. Further, the *antecedents* of material poverty are *non-material*; they, too, are *spiritual*. In order to explain that, we must turn to consideration of religious principles. As the society of Henry George and others of us in a number of western societies was based on the life and teachings of Jesus, it is to that teaching that I turn for our considerations of poverty.

Poverty

Poverty is a central theme of the Bible – both the Old and New Testaments – and of major world religions. According to Gustavo Gutierrez in his seminal text, *A Theology of Liberation* (Richard Clay publishers U.K., 1988), poverty is both a 'scandalous condition' *materially*, (italics mine), and 'spiritual childhood' (p. 165). The first – the 'scandalous condition' – is, of course, a negative. The second – 'spiritual childhood' – is a positive. Wisdom literature tells us we are spiritual beings and, thus, to become mature we must engage with the spiritual essence of our common humanity; open ourselves with the innocence of 'children' and engage with the Spirit of Truth from our own spiritual position of humility, willingness, and availability. Poverty as a 'scandalous condition' will never be eliminated unless we acknowledge and transform our human immaturity into 'spiritual childhood'; into childlike humility, powerlessness (which turns out to be actually *powerfulness*), willingness, availability, trust in the Great Mysterious Reality that many call 'God'.

Successive parliaments remonstrate, legislate, devise programs, throw money at, rationalise, blame their predecessors, justify and engage in all manner of other useless strategies, and poverty continues unabated and increases in spread and depth. The 'scandalous condition' is brought about through policies created by, and favouring, the wealthy and influential 'immature' humans – our 'leaders' and their corporate masters –who are either ignorant of the need, or too arrogant to submit to, becoming, 'spiritual *children*' and, thus wise and compassionate, egalitarian, true leaders.

As detailed by Simone Weil in her belief that all political parties should be abolished, well-meaning political party members cannot not lie; their allegiance to the party agenda forces them to adopt a myopic view of societal organisation, effectively suppressing any chance of required transformation to *fair*. The requirement to transform the material aspect of the 'scandalous condition' has been well described and uncontestably argued by spiritual and other humanitarian leaders throughout history.

Economically, for 150 years, innumerable people have attempted to have the Georgist paradigm accepted as the essential change for fairness. Even though there is a steady and growing exodus from membership of the major political parties, there seems little impetus even amongst the growing number of independent political representatives to either recognise or promote George's assertion that moving away from private ownership of land

105

resources is the only way for public finance to become fair; the only way for provision to be equitable for all and actually democratic. And for the scandalous gulf between Indigenous and non-Indigenous to be eliminated!

The *spiritual childhood* aspect of liberation to fairness is another story altogether, and it seems, similarly, that there is little awareness of, or interest in, eliminating material poverty from that direction. Of course, the *scandalous condition* and *spiritual childhood* can't be considered in isolation from one another; they are inextricable aspects of the one malady; our refusal to surrender to our Inner Reality which is life-giving Love. If by some miracle, the reorganisation of public finance became *legislated* to be *fair*, the *spiritual childhood* would not necessarily be increased. On the contrary, if by some arguably greater miracle a spiritual transformation swept humanity, and we all became as '*spiritual children*', the scandalous condition would readily dissolve.

Unlearning and Relearning

Does that indicate where our education and socialisation efforts need to be placed? Should we be turning our attention away from over-focus on the physical aspects of life, and towards the arguably more-significant spiritual awareness and practice? Where the latter is the focus of women and men, great humanitarian movements are created and sustained. Where the example, teaching, and *indwelling presence* of the historic/cosmic Christ Spirit are being lived by people, truth, justice and the public good are practised. Something ineffable yet demonstrably real about the mysterious, transcendent – and – immanent Spirit of God – of oneness with all that is and of justice, mercy and compassion – is required to be awakened in each of us for life on planet earth to work; to survive and thrive; to be fair to all life and especially including the life of the earth-organism. Of course, the flawed- human organisation of Christianity has not been very good at embodying the Christ-Spirit of Oneness in Love. Much Christian experience for the last 500 years or so has been focused more on the historic, *'bearded and sandalled Jesus'* (Josh McDowell, *More Than A Carpenter*, Elam Ministries 2010) than on radical surrender to, and experience of, the transcendent, universal, eternal 'Christ-Image' that each human being already contains, albeit mostly unacknowledged and unlived.

That Tricky 'E' Word

It's not possible to consider change without mentioning the ego; that essential human quality dealing with the day to day interactions with all aspects of living as human beings. Noted above, and more comprehensively in my recent book, *Uncommon Sense: reclaiming humanity*, the ego is not qualified to be the executive of the person. That's the task for the deeper self – the spirit/soul; that part of us we might call the 'God' part.

It's worth remembering that wisdom says, *'it is a fool who says in his heart "there is no God"'* (Psalm 14:1). But, oh, what trouble we have in accepting the proposition that there may be some entity – some mysterious, life-giving force underpinning the entire universe – that/who is greater than me! Greater than my little ego! Those who refuse to consider, reflect upon, accept and submit to that other authority, however, are those of us who remain bereft of Gutierrez' *spiritual childhood*. Such submission is considered by many to be a weakness of character; weak people who need a crutch. The reverse is actually the truth. Being prepared to '*do the will of another rather than your own will*' (Brother Lawrence, *The Practice of the Presence of God*, Martino Fine Books, 2016), the will of a community, for example (Rousseau's *general will*), takes greater strength, character and wisdom than doing your own thing; than selfishly exercising your own *particular will*. And, paradoxically, it produces an actual experience of strength and control for one's life, and is demonstrably so in subsequent actions.

Immature humans are *reactive*. Those receptive to the reality of the *inner light* of Spirit, and who allow that spirit to empower and lead, are *reflective* and *proactive*. They are those who have embraced their '*spiritual childhood*' and are embracing the process of human maturity – an ongoing process for the duration of life.

Conclusion
How will our story end?

How will our story end? That depends on us individually and communally; on our values, our beliefs, our political, economic and social structures, on what we focus and value, and where we place our energies. I suspect our story will end badly if we don't *wake up*, learn from the folly of some of our forebears, recognise indications of the same in ourselves and some of our contemporaries, and transform the way we think and act. We need only to reflect on the eventual decline and demise of every great civilisation throughout history to get an insight into our destination if we continue on the path of unawareness or blatant abuse of the sanctity and equality of our human nature; if we passively accept oppression and coercion, injustice and dealing carelessly with – or, more accurately, denying – 'truth'.

Reform

Successive governments in Australia talk about reform. Whilst they may be well-meant statements of intent, there is nothing of substance to indicate there exists any grounds for optimism that reform will be achieved. In fact, the reverse is the case. Whilst the social, economic and political health-indicators continue as they are on a downward trajectory, there has been and is no 'reform'. Reform requires a radical departure from that which is taking us in a negative direction.

First and foremost, reform requires that the government of the day has control of public finance. Governments in Australia don't! Privatisation of essential public assets (some of our food production, water and mineral resources, power generation, communications, transport, I.T. technologies, etc.), deregulation and private ownership of the banking system, laws allowing profits made here to leave the country, laws allowing corporate profits here to be offset against losses elsewhere resulting in no tax being paid in Australia (hundreds of multi-million dollar companies pay not one cent of tax in Australia), laws allowing ecological destruction with little responsibility to restore exploited areas, the list goes on.

Reform requires new rules; new rules governing the production and distribution of the goods necessary for a life of dignity and security for all citizens. New rules governing access to the nation's resources *provided freely by God for the benefit of all creatures'* (with apologies for the repetition of something we need to take on board); rules that put an appropriate value on resources and prevent private persons from freely appropriating them for their personal benefit. I've said earlier, for something like 60,000 years, Australian Aborigines demonstrated the egalitarian efficacy of *'land custodianship by community'* instead of *'land ownership by private individuals'*. The former inspired; the latter perhaps well-meaning unaware, unfair and unsustainable.

Reform demands new rules governing the political structure to eliminate the scourge of partisan interest and the lobbyists and political donors ensuring such interest. Reform demands a politics of *disinterest*; a structure of ethical leadership that affects the good of *all* citizens and all of creation rather than for the diminishing few the present system benefits through the private ownership of public resources. Reform demands new rules abolishing the dysfunctional, impotent, wasteful, unfair party system that forces members to deny their consciences, lie, and be effectively prevented from seeking justice and the public good. And reform involves each of us reflecting on our personal values, attitudes and actions, and the impact of those on others and on the life of the earth. Reform demands that we recognise the connection between our destructive land use and the growing number and intensity of extreme weather events around the world.

At the time of writing, the East Coast of Australia – particularly New South Wales and Queensland – was being devastated by hundreds of wild-fires. Several thousand dwellings have been destroyed together with 7 million hectares of bushland habitat and, equally tragically, untold *billions* of creatures of every description. The climate has changed. The environment has changed. Post- colonial human activity is largely responsible for that change. We haven't learned what we need to know about living successfully in this land.

In his inspiring book, *Dark Emu* (Magabala Books, Western Australia, 2014), a truthful rewrite of early colonial history, Bruce Pascoe reminds us that the archaeological record shows that the wild-fires as we know them today did not occur during the land management of the Aboriginal people. They had learned to use fire as a tool, an ally. They had no fear of it because they knew when to burn, selectively where and how much to burn, how to ensure cool burns that controlled understorey and prevented the possibility of crowning fires that are increasingly devastating in the Australia of today.

Our European fear of fire results from our cultural failure to understand how our land use practices and fire are to be considered in concert. Our private ownership, arbitrary clearing, fencing, cropping and stocking with non-indigenous species, building and protection of all that infrastructure has meant that the judicious, regionally and nationally coordinated use of cool burns is not universally possible.

Consequently, we end up with high fuel loads of understorey, inaccessibility, dramatic lack of moisture in soil and vegetation, and a recipe for fire disasters that will continue. Yet still the government is allowing forests to be cleared; trees that sequester carbon that otherwise enters the atmosphere; trees that transpire desperately-needed moisture into the atmosphere and soil thus moderating the micro-climate and encouraging rainfall; trees that provide livelihoods for myriad creatures sustaining the intricate web of life in the eco-systems and, ultimately, our lives as well. Reform demands that we re-evaluate all of our farming and land and water use practices to re-establish the sustainability of life in Australia that existed pre-colonialism.

Thinking of the tragic impact we 'newer-comers' have had both on this land and its ancient people (and yes, we all too, *belong* to this beautiful land), drew me to write these song lyrics: 'What Have We Done' (2008).

What have we done, what have we done to the people
of this land?
We didn't watch, we didn't listen, we didn't learn
what we needed to know.
For life here to grow, as it grew for sixty thousand
years...'til we came here.
What have we done, what have we done to the land
of this people?
We didn't taste, we didn't smell, we didn't feel the
abundance that was here.
We planted grass where there were trees, we cleared
and grazed this country to its knees.
What have we done, what have we done everywhere
we've ever been?
We didn't celebrate the beauty; we changed the look
of everything to be seen
Have we lost our souls completely, or have we just
forgotten who we are?
What have we done, what have we done to the lives
of men and women?
We depress not elevate them, we neglect and we
berate them, we are fools.
We ignore and we abuse, we mislead and we confuse
them with our rules.

What have we done, what have we done to so many
of our children?
We neglect, we violate them, disaffect them and we
break them.
One more sin... and we annihilate them, we end their
lives before they begin.
What have I done, what have I done to the spirit that
is me?
I look out instead of in, I am drowning in sin, I've lost
the way.
Think I'm up, I'm really down, I am lost but think I'm
found .
I'm in my mind and not my heart, and I'm tearing me
apart.
What have I done? What have we done?
It's getting late, very late, but while there's breath it's
not too late to move.
It's very late, but not too late, to leave the path of fear
and reach for love

The bottom line for our decision-making is this: *if the
earth can't afford it, we can't have it!* Reform would produce
considerable disruption and temporary discomfort for
many of us. But, unless we endure that, future generations
may not have a future, and this beautiful earth will be in
deep trouble. Any discomfort that comes with reform also
brings new opportunities for creativity and diversity that
energise and produce health for citizens, and cause a new
phoenix to rise from the ashes.

The most necessary reform is both the least acknowledged
as being valid and, because of the inflated ego of our
post-modern and immature approach to life, the most
difficult to imagine being attained: *the transformation of the*

unsubmitted human heart from whence comes every evil that has ever beset the human race and the world of exquisite beauty and wonder. How our story will end depends entirely on each of us acknowledging the truth about ourselves as eternal spirit/Love – beings existing in a brief physical experience we know as 'life'. Throughout all human history, much has been thought and spoken about life. Religions and philosophies proliferate, ideas and opinions abound. Confusion and fear remain prominent in all unaware, unconscious, un-surrendered lives, and continue to destroy the magnificence of the natural world and all its amazing life-forms. We human beings are just one of those life forms. All other life-forms – including the very life of the planet itself – depend, for their continued existence and function, on our actions.

Ultimately, our **'making Australia fair'** – our waking up to truth, justice and the good for all life – is primarily dependent upon our being *drawn* to the truth about us; on our recognition of who we truly are – creatures of the earth itself powered by the Spirit of Love, the Spirit of 'God' (Wisdom literature tells us that 'God is Love'), the Transcendent, Immanent Spirit of the One the earth knew for a few brief years of history, and will know for all time to come, as the God-man, Jesus Christ. Not Christianity or Church, but the real thing; the humble Love-Truth-Spirit in action in our lives. That presents each of us with an issue that needs to be addressed: what will our personal response be? Whilst this is not the place for any attempt to do justice to the person of Jesus of Nazareth, this man said and did some amazing things – things that no other human being has said or done before or since.

Arguably the most significant is that he said that he was more than just another man. He claimed to have been with God from the beginning of creation. He was acknowledged and known as Son of Man, Son of God, Saviour of the World, the Holy One of Israel, Redeemer of Humankind. That mystery is impossible to get our heads around, because our heads are finite and the mystery is infinite! Remember it is the little ego that demands understanding. If we achieved that, we would be equal to God. Not an option! Thankfully.

In the New Testament, we can read accounts of that remarkable, singular life. We can read them in a detached fashion as interesting stories of long ago, and choose to dismiss them. We have *free will* – instructively a characteristic for which we can't claim credit. We can choose whether or not to accede to these stories as truth. Of course, much of humankind has been resisting that accession for thousands of years, and the disastrous results can be seen everywhere humans are to be found. Our central challenge remains: what do we personally and, thus, corporately, do with that historic revelation? Can this matter be likened to the force of gravity which can be demonstrated but not dismissed? Citing hypocrisy, sexual and psychological abuse, anti-intellectualism and a host of other 'justifications', many individuals have found reason to reject the established Church.

The tragedy is that that the Christ-Presence of Truth and Love is rejected with it. The baby with the bathwater. The organisation of 'church' has much to answer for in its incompetence to appropriately and effectively communicate the Truth that each one of us is seeking in one way or another but don't readily see in many organisations of Christianity. This is not to blame, but to point up the common human frailty of us all as we struggle to contain the spiritual with the physical in some kind of dynamic tension, and choose the former to be the executive of the latter.

A Miracle Needed

It would truly be a miracle of God for our resistance to cease. We often have, and can continue to hope for such a miracle, for nothing else – which we have tried and at which have dismally failed – has so far proven to be of any real value. But it seems clear that hope is not enough; we need to do more than just hope. People the world over throughout all of history have had hope. Often that hope was accompanied by desperation and anxiety. But some – the humble and wise – to their hope have added deep awareness, present moment consciousness, stillness and silence, surrendered *'being-with-what-is'*, and that *inner light* referred to by Simone Weil and many others.

That's the miracle! This deep prayer produces the experience of 'oneness with all that is' and a sense of quiet, secure, buoyant peace. Many have prayed and hoped as if it all depended on God. Many others have done that, and also worked as if it all depended on them. Perhaps a combination of both is required. Of course, that requires serious engagement with this particular focus of reality, and the gift of spiritual insight that leads to the necessary *surrender* of that troublesome ego which torments ourselves and our world. This *'surrender'* – a huge and crucial subject for another time and place – is a gift that is to be both received and chosen. And this *gift* is on offer! This miracle is available! Will we consider, open ourselves to, and receive it is the question that underlies whether or not we are *willing* to 'wake up' and commit to becoming 'fair' in Australia and elsewhere, to fullness of life as it was intended for all creatures.

Afterword

> What has been will be again,
> What has been done, will be done again,
> there is nothing new under the sun.
>
> *(Ecclesiastes 1:9)*

I offer the following – none of which is new but much of which I believe we need to remind ourselves – with an apology for any nuisance value in stating the obvious. This little book – '**Making Australia Fair** – is a rambling attempt to turn our efforts towards making life satisfying and meaningful for all. As outlined above, if we have the spiritual and common- sense insight – and we each already have access internally to both – and if we have the courage and commitment to democratic humanity for Australia, delight is eminently possible. For every one of us.

Remember, our Aboriginal sisters and brothers lived that simple delight for 60,000 years or so. In the very recent past, these sisters and brothers offered Australia a great gift. That gift was and is the *Uluru Statement from the Heart*. After comprehensive consultation across the nation, Aboriginal elders offered us all a pathway towards healing of the terrible wounds of the past; a pathway to becoming a healthy, whole, single nation honouring our common humanity, and honouring wisdom and compassion, ancient and modern, to immeasurably-enrich earth-life for all. To this point, the 'Voice' of Australia's First Peoples has not been heard or honoured by Parliament. And it must be. This most pressing responsibility is to listen deeply and equally to the voices of our Aboriginal sisters and brothers, and humbly and diligently act to achieve radical, inclusive honouring. It is unconscionable that we allow this 'offer of wisdom and grace' not to be humbly and formally recognised constitutionally, politically, economically and socially.

Restoring the Flow

There are simple, delightful practicalities that will automatically flow from repairing the fatal flaws in Neo-Classical Economics and the Party-Political System of government. And government and economists must be assisted to realise that, without radical departure from the current fatally-dysfunctional systems, there can be no satisfaction for all. There can be no justice for all. No government can claim to be 'successful'. Successive governments' fine sounding words – and probably genuinely meant – about 'closing the gap' between non-indigenous and Aboriginal peoples are just that; fine sounding, vapid, impotent words that will fail as all previous similar sentiments in this matter have failed.

The still-widening 'gap' that is more like a 'chasm' is not possible to close because the playing field is not level. It has huge holes in it. The rules are unfair. They favour the tiny, privileged minority of wealthy and influential. In fact, it is not only our Aboriginal sisters and brothers who are separated from dignity by a chasm. All but the elite few who make and keep the rules are separated. The majority of us. As we elect our governments, this inequity is in our control. It is up to all of us to exercise personal and corporate responsibility to monitor government policies and activities, and actively engage to ensure outcomes for the public good.

The Opportunity

The growing climate crisis is presenting many people – especially our young people – with debilitating anxiety, depression, despair, damaging lives and relationships at an increasingly alarming rate. With political accession to the provision of a 'job guarantee', that suffering and waste could be truncated. This crisis is also presenting us with an enormous opportunity. Because Australia is rich in renewable energy resources of solar, wind, pumped-hydro, hydrogen, land geo-sequestration, we could be positioned to become a zero-emission nation by 2030.

And that is only the beginning. In his 2019 book *Super-Power*, (LaTrobe University Press), senior economist and professional fellow of the University of Melbourne, Ross Garnaut, details how Australia could develop renewable energy technologies to transform energy, transport and agriculture, together with vastly-expanded domestic and global industry, priced to be easily-competitive in world markets. All we lack at present is the political will.

Our present government is stuck on a 'gas-led (fossil-fuel) Covid-recovery' – a ridiculous proposal according to climate and energy experts, and in the light of the immense renewable energy resources available in this country.

When *land* is separated from *capital*, and when the resources of that land (and water and air) that are the rightful property of all citizens are no longer able to be quarantined for personal benefit of the wealthy and powerful few, then and only then will justice for all begin. Democracy will have arrived. 'Egalitarianism', 'Communitarianism', 'True Socialism', or some other yet-to-be-formulated arrangement will have replaced Capitalism. Capitalism has failed to deliver a civil society. Masses of citizens miss out on the basics. Similarly, as they have been corrupted by *coercive* force, Socialism and Communism have also failed to deliver.

It would be of benefit for our would-be leaders of the future to consider the contribution of thinkers such as Antonio Gramsci, 1891-1937, an Italian 'Neo-Marxist' philosopher and politician. He believed unequivocally that Socialism was the future, but not in its 'usually-implemented form' of coercive state ownership and control. Gramsci correctly saw that, because of human free-will, people refuse to be *driven* by external force; they must be *drawn* from within themselves. He saw that the future depends on *'the formation of a collective will...forming habits in collective man that make social behaviour automatic'* (in Eric Hobsbawn, *How to Change The World*, Yale University Press, 2012). His understanding was that *socialisation* of the whole person is the key to successful, workable Socialism and a civil society. Although expressed in more secular terms, Gramsci's vision seems to be harmonious with what we've been discussing above in spiritual terms. Effective socialisation of the human person surely requires 'both/and' rather than 'either/or'. We are *One* individually and communally. Secular and spiritual belong together as expressions of that *One*; the physical inextricably-intermixed with the spiritual.

If we follow the above line of thinking about developing a civil and fair society rather than leaving it to markets alone to dictate, wages and benefits would be set by government at levels preventing poverty and disadvantage. (Even the Australian business community is saying that Newstart needs to be lifted $100 per week to bring it up to a mere subsistence level.) As it is in some social-democratic countries in Europe, education at all levels will be free, and sufficiently flexible to accommodate needs current, emerging, and projected, and for the 'whole person'. The curricula will be permeated by physical, intellectual, spiritual, philosophical, existential components as is the case in a growing number of Northern European countries, and was in some early democracies.

Re-education

Our education system focuses too much on ego cleverness and physical prowess, inhibiting or dismissing the development of *inner light* of the spirit, the teaching of the *source of goodness*, and the equal valuing of all gifts. In the Northern European nation of Denmark, for example – although focus on spiritual matters is similar to that in Australian schools

–children spend fewer hours in formal classrooms than Australian children, have longer play hours, no homework, less focus on competition, and comprehensive, less formal assessments avoiding the stress of 'performance'. Ironically, in that deregulated environment, students' performance is considerably superior on most measures to that of our Aussie kids locked into our failed 'Naplan' system of standardised testing, long hours in classroom, lots of homework, little value placed on the creative arts and wholesome human relationships. (Not to mention the unacceptable pressures placed on our heroic teachers). And those Danish kids are happier and better adjusted than are ours.

Women

Not that any country is without its problems and flaws, but it is demonstrated in countries including Sweden, Finland, Denmark and Iceland, to be socially secure and 'happy' as a nation, it is essential common sense to recognise the indispensable contribution that only women can make, and celebrate women as equal partners in respect and in every aspect of government and social leadership. Whatever the religious or philosophical stance a woman may take, she is generally more able than a man to contact and engage with her truest, spiritual essence; the mysterious reality that is nurturing, equalising, life-giving love.

Women are 'soft-wired' to care, protect, include, negotiate, conciliate, heal, forgive, share, feel and value human dignity more readily than are men. Those crucial human qualities are in addition to their abilities – equal to any man

– to manage, control, direct, build, develop, grow and sustain governments, corporations and organisations of all descriptions; qualities that transform and maximise humanity wherever they are encouraged to be. It is heartening to see the increasing emergence of women in government and community leadership and corporate office in some of the more enlightened countries.

Unfortunately for Australia, we are still dragging our feet in this regard. Of CEOs appointed to twenty-five of Australia's top companies, only one is a woman. Women are more likely to talk than shoot; women, generally, seek peaceful rather than powerful existence. Of course, peaceful is, *actually*, powerful. It is instructive to note that women were held in the highest regard in Aboriginal society, and in the role of authority to direct, secure, nurture and sustain family and inter-group relationships. Non-Aboriginal woman are still waiting for their indispensable, unique gifts to be acknowledged, valued, remunerated and integrated into a society languishing because of their absence from the centre. In order to develop an affordable life of dignity for all, Australia needs the *anima* – the 'feminine principle'– the inclusive, gentle, nurturing, life-giving principle – to be much more acknowledged, valued and peacefully/dynamically present both in women and – especially – in men.

Inappropriate Metrics

We need to abandon as an indicator of our nation's success the measure of GDP alone. As a generality, most GDP increase ends up in the same few bank accounts of the wealthy and influential. Stalled wages growth, unemployment and underemployment, increasing depression, anxiety and despair, rising numbers of homeless, rising prison populations significantly linked to poverty, insufficient funding of health, welfare and education services are some of the actual indicators that the GDP numbers are of little use other than as 'spin' for the incumbent government.

The Chief Economist at the Australia Institute, Richard Denniss, correctly states that the *shape* of the economy is of far greater significance than the *size*. Our government has been and remains far too small to effectively provide for the needs of all citizens. As mentioned earlier, functional government requires willingness to spend whatever is required in order to provide essential infrastructure, ensure full employment, with adequate wage level set by government rather than by the 'market', and an appropriate 'care economy' staffed by government employees. For decades, our governments have been obsessed with the irrelevant and socially-damaging aim of avoiding budget deficits, wrongly assuming that deficits are 'bad'. Visionary government economists have demonstrated time and again in post-war periods and cyclical financial crises that deficit spending balances the economy; avoids mass unemployment, develops essential services and infrastructure, controls inflation and improves quality of life for all citizens.

Domestic and national Security

For a people to be content and secure, a strong, sustainable local and domestic economy is required ahead of global economic reliance; a domestic economy that manufactures and provides the majority of what is needed to maintain a secure and affordable life of dignity and purpose for all. Although not being austere, dull and colourless, manufacturing needs to be primarily for *needs* first rather than consumer gimmicks and *wants* that merely consume the finite resources of this beautiful earth, and distract us from the deeper purpose of profound, mature, inclusive humanity. Recent events of the devastating bushfires, and the current Corona Virus pandemic, are testament to the folly of relying on international supply chains, exports and tourism as fundamentals of economic stability.

Sovereignty

To maintain sovereignty, control of Australian assets by foreign owners must be rolled back and disallowed; it is merely common sense to ensure Australians maintain control of Australia's assets, security, resources and essential services. For too long, we have accepted politicians talking up the benefits of *foreign investment* which, in reality, is foreign *ownership and control*. Focus on wealth creation – which accumulates in fewer bank accounts and never 'trickles down' as those who have it want us to believe – has resulted in many Australians becoming hard and brittle, as we struggle to make for ourselves and our families, a life of dignity and sufficiency.

As a nation, we have unwittingly allowed control of our lives to be transferred to the few with wealth and influence to make and sustain rules that benefit them; fatally-flawed rules that, as we've discussed above, are unsustainable and unfair. The few with wealth and influence have distracted many politicians from their role of governing and providing necessary services to *all* citizens. There is much to change here, and the principles and strategies for such change have been available and detailed by 'Georgists', for example, for a very long time. For a very much longer time those principles have been practised by our Aboriginal people who wisely saw that land cannot be owned.

Responsibility

Essential public health care services providing safety, economy and dignity for the duration of life are the responsibility of government. The fact that so many essential community services fall to *volunteers* to provide, is an indictment of government that fails to effectively utilise the nation's rich resources and sovereign currency for the benefit of all citizens.

However much government and private enterprise protest to the contrary, private enterprise is generally unable and unwilling to put quality of care ahead of share-holder expectations and the profit motive. At the time of writing, that obscene reality is being brought home to us in the unfolding disaster that is the under-resourced, private and not-for-profit aged care facilities in which the vast majority of deaths have occurred. The 'care economy' has been disgracefully neglected for decades by both 'sides' of government. As mentioned earlier, a 'federal job guarantee', both desirable and affordable, could have averted the present disaster by accepting responsibility for *all* citizens, rather than leaving 1.5 million citizens without livelihoods.

Covid-19 would have stopped many from working, but none from being financially secure.

Responsible government would prohibit import of any non-recyclable materials, and own and operate waste transformation facilities; accept responsibility for governing this vital aspect of community life. Railways should be revitalised, upgraded and owned by the public, and road transport restricted where rail is available. Obviously, road services need to be provided as necessity dictates in remote locations.

Control of Public Finances

Financial institutions need to be effectively regulated in order for government to be in control of public funding. Money to provide public services doesn't need to be borrowed at interest, nor does it need to come from taxes, because the Australian government has the authority to issue and spend Australian dollars into the economy. It is simply not true that government can't afford x or y essential service. Political leaders seem not to understand how finance works, as they continue to obsess about the size of the deficit and seek to place arbitrary limits that prevent the provision of essential services – especially in youth, health and aged care.

Further, an obscene example of government not being in control of finance, we have the ridiculous legal situation that allows corporations to sue government – to sue the tax payer – for loss of income due to government policy. Corporations pressure politicians to enact laws that lock citizens into practices that are fail-safe for the corporations. Until there's a financial crash requiring a 'bail out'. If government was competent in 'functional finance' and focused on balancing the economy rather than the budget, financial crises could be averted or drastically mitigated.

Accommodation

Cities need to be limited in size, and government services, production, manufacture, and distribution need to be effectively decentralised. 'Efficiency' needs to be replaced by 'effectiveness'! Efficiency is generally about profit; effectiveness is generally about dignity of all humanity and life on earth, and about moderate and considered consumption of resources. Our earlier discussion about the immediate development of our vast renewable energy opportunities would easily achieve such decentralisation and effectiveness of governance.

Adequate, affordable public housing needs to be provided by government to ensure that citizens of limited means are afforded dignity. Speculation, private developments and negative gearing on domestic dwellings need to be phased out in order for house prices not to be inflated beyond the means of all who wish to purchase a home. It has been demonstrated by Georgists that a single tax on land would achieve that. The replacement of private ownership of land with rent of the same would achieve that. *Importantly it would also put every Australian in right relationship with land; in awareness that it is from the land that we draw our very substance and existence, a fact known and lived for millennia by Aboriginal peoples.* We didn't learn from them. And they, and all of us, and the beautiful land itself, now suffer because of our folly, unwitting and deliberate; because of our continuing unawareness and/or arrogance.

Livelihoods

A living wage or some similar arrangement – a federal 'job guarantee' mentioned earlier – and a life of dignity for all, could easily be afforded if government required those who benefit from the exploitation of natural resources to pay the value of those resources into the public fund as is done to a greater extent in Norway for example. A vast public fund has accumulated in that nation to provide adequate services, and as a hedge against unforeseen future circumstances. Education in public institutions – including universities – is free even for overseas students. Australia, blessed with vast natural resources, should be enjoying the most buoyant financial circumstances of any country on earth. There should be no poverty, no homelessness, no need for desperate criminal activity to either provide for a life of dignity or to beat meaninglessness, disillusionment and despair. How is it acceptable that around a million Australian children are living in poverty in one of the resource-richest nations on earth! How can that be allowed?

If we but repaired the Neo-Classical Economic flaw crippling the present systems of creation and distribution of wealth – that is, if we separated *land* from *capital* – *and* eliminated or, at least limited, private ownership and control of land, air and water resources, most of the maladies besetting an increasing majority of Australian citizens would be resolved. Justice and equity would prevail. Everyone would be better off. The wealthy would be less wealthy but would suffer no privation. And if we were to abolish the present wasteful, adversarial, impotent Party-Political system of government, we would enter an era in which truth, justice and the public good, i.e. actual democracy, would prevail. The only question is, will the few who benefit most from what God has given freely for *all* to enjoy, open themselves to *inner light* and realise the gross and unacceptable unfairness of their benefits? And will the rest of us – Australians all – becoming aware of the inequity in the economic and political systems, refuse to accept their inevitability, and actively, non-violently yet persistently *engage* in order to radically transform those unjust systems of our nation and world? Such transformation is actually the obligation, and within the personal resources, of each of us!

What went Wrong?

We might ask, '*How did we go so wrong to be in the mess we are today?* There is a simple answer, but one that, with our burgeoning cleverness and illusory sophistication, is increasingly unpopular. The answer is in Wisdom literature, notably including the Bible, The Upanishads, The Bhagavad Gita, Buddhist Sutras, writings of mystics throughout history that too few of us read and even fewer consider and follow. The Bible calls it *sin*, and it can be described as '*a breach of friendship with God and others, and the ultimate cause of poverty, injustice and the oppression in which persons live*' (Gustavo Gutierrez, *A Theology of Liberation*, Orbis Books, 1988). That breach has also been described by some in terms such as *our failure to realise our humble yet profound value as 'loved beings', belonging to and with and in the 'Essential Oneness' of Life that is Love/Truth/Ground of Being/God and many other terms unable to ever effectively represent that to which they point.* Only realising, engaging, and surrendering to that deepest inner Reality – our *existential* reality – can we begin living our design – living completely free, unattached to our opinions, possessions, ideas, values, achievements; unphased by both pleasure and pain, inclusive of all others and all of creation.

Our wilful *and* unwitting departure from revealed wisdom and truth has put us at odds with the principles and practices that make life work; that make life equitable; fair for all people, all creatures and for the earth itself.

Wisdom literature provides the antidote for our personal and collective *failure*. It is simply to *repent*, another uncomfortable word actually meaning to *rethink, reconsider, be convicted, and choose to act in radically different ways*. The only difficulty for us is that our often-inflated egos – our unconscious, dualistic minds – are extremely reluctant to admit fault of any sort. And extremely reluctant to consider there may be some mysterious entity or power greater than me! But there is no other way forward. As we've said before, the ego – although essential in its role of day-to-day interactions with the externals of being alive – is not qualified to *direct our lives in right ways*. That direction is the role of the spirit – the *inner light* we've talked about – that deepest place within us that is able to hear a challenge, discern truth, and to choose a new path; a path that considers others and all other aspects of the created order as inextricably *'one with ourselves'*, and interacts with them accordingly.

The unjust structures of Neo-Classical Economics and Party Politics are expressions of our personal and collective sin of alienation from God, self, others and the earth, and our associated, culpable acceptance of oppression. These unjust structures are primarily responsible for the unfairness in our social organisation. These are the structures of which we need to repent; to radically turn away from and absolutely reject. There is another way for us to be on earth together; a fairer way. We simply and responsibly need to inform ourselves of it, engage with it, and *require* those who would 'lead' us to do the same.

'Radical reform' is essential! Reform of the very *radicals* – the roots – of our systems; reform that demands an end to the Neo-Liberal ideology of small government, privatisation of government responsibilities and public assets, so-called 'free-trade', and reliance on 'the markets' to direct economic management and public policy. Over several decades in Australia, both sides of politics have blindly subscribed to the absolute folly of privatising essential public services, and cutting those services until they are not able to function adequately. For example, increasingly over recent decades, waiting times to speak to someone on the phone have become unacceptable simply because government has no control over telecommunications, and there are too few people employed to answer phones. And this whilst hundreds of thousands are unemployed.

That inadequacy of function becomes frighteningly evident when a crisis such as the current Coronavirus arrives. We are not well prepared for such crises, even though we have experienced epidemics and pandemics throughout history. Influenzas, Cholera, Yellow Fever, Ebola, Swine Flu, Meningitis, Legionnaire's, Spanish Flu, HIV-AIDS – hundreds of millions have succumbed to microscopic enemies. And now, Covid-19 has killed hundreds of thousands in a few short weeks. After such dramatic demonstrations of what viruses can do to humanity, one might think that a greater focus would be on securing health and community well-being rather than ramping up military expenditure to 'protect us', and keeping partisan ideology front and centre.

Decades of Neo-Liberal neglect and political leadership inadequacy have seen this magnificent, rich country and its people cruelly and avoidably wounded. Essential services have been stripped to the bone, employment has been casualised and contracturalised, making millions vulnerable to the present crisis, free-trade has replaced fair trade and made us dependent on a small number of international suppliers; we export raw materials and import virtually everything we need for day to day life. Successive governments have been blindsided by an unwise obsession with growth, somehow believing that a big number is a success, but failing to acknowledge the shape of government that spreads the wealth of resources and human talent across the workforce, resulting in a sustainable livelihood arrangement within the control of the nation and not dependent on the vicissitudes of international commerce. No-one should be left behind in times of plenty or times of difficulty.

Until this Covid-19 crisis demanded primary attention, we'd been driven into the ground by a government obsessed with the irrelevant goal of producing a surplus at a time when money is as cheap as it's ever been – that's if we *had* to borrow which, as a 'currency-issuing nation', we don't have to do. Wages are stagnated, unemployment is unacceptably high, associated depression, despair, domestic violence and incarceration are on the increase. Present government is driven by ideology that has no resemblance to true 'liberalism', the original meaning of which in government is 'fairness for all'. We urgently need to *wake up*; to realise we've been following a path to national disintegration. Our wasteful, adversarial, dishonest political structure has failed and must be replaced. Our market-driven, wealth and power focused economic arrangements have also failed and must be transformed to become just and sustainable. However, it is likely that neither of those two essential 'reforms' will occur unless and until we realise who we really are as *spiritual beings* whose Central and True Self is 'life-giving Love'; that Love needs to be submitted to as the guide and primary motivator of all that we are and do in the world.

The absence of that love has been graphically brought to us in the shocking murders of two African American men by police. This disgraceful display of violence – this evil disregard for the rights and well-being of a fellow human – has rightly shocked the world into joining in condemnation of the brutality of police violence and racism. Of course, the fact of the American love-affair with firearms has created an environment in which police, too, are in fear for their lives and constantly on edge. The right to bear arms needs to be rescinded. The cry of 'black lives matter' echoes around the world. All lives matter, and are to be equally valued! Our history of racism here in Australia is, in some ways, worse than that of the United States. Our rates of incarceration of our indigenous sisters and brothers are several times higher than that of African Americans in the U.S.

In Australia, our history of gross injustice for indigenous people is, and will remain, an enduring disgrace for us all until this scourge of human violation is redressed. Almost a third of our male prison population is indigenous and, even more- shockingly, 36% of the female prison population is indigenous! And this in a group of citizens that is only 3% of our national population! In 1991, the Royal Commission into Aboriginal Deaths in Custody released a number of recommendations. Twenty-nine years later, 40% of those recommendations have not been implemented. And since 1991, there have been a further 432 aboriginal deaths in custody. Not a single conviction of police or prison officials in some way responsible, has resulted. In recent days, a white public servant convicted of a serious involvement in fraud was given a short custodial sentence which was suspended. Around the same time, an Aboriginal woman convicted of a petty infringement was jailed.

We might wonder how can this be called a democracy? How can this systemic failure not be redressed?

Repossession of Personhood

It is just possible, of course, that the present social turmoil of violence and racism, and Covid-19 pandemic may continue to force government to realise that, for our entire post-colonial history, we have accepted our dispossession of Aboriginal people and the resultant destruction and disadvantage of that rich and valuable cultural group of our sisters and brothers. And for our entire post-colonial history, government public sector has been far too small to sustain lives of integrity and stability for the majority of citizens. A new experience of appropriate, adequate, *just* provision for the entire population may come to be seen to be both essential and practical; it just may precipitate an abandonment of the failed ideology of small, sectarian government and too much reliance upon the self-focused, greed-driven nature of the private sector, and upon the mighty army of unheralded, unselfish volunteers without whom this nation would sink entirely into a deathly morass.

To prevent such a decline, it is perhaps instructive to consider three of the most transformative words we can use: 'I am responsible'. We are often tempted to point a finger and blame someone or some entity when things are not as we would like them to be. I've talked a lot here about failure of political and economic systems, and the destructive effects those failures have on social organisation. The failures are real. And they are failures by people in positions of leadership and power; people whom *we* have elected to lead us.

If there is responsibility to be ascribed – and there always is – is it not reasonable that we should consider *ourselves* responsible for our choices of leaders and policies? Is it not reasonable to accept personal and collective responsibility for our inadequate engagement with the political, economic and social processes? That our lack of awareness, interest and action are jointly responsible for the problems in our societies? That perhaps we've neglected our own, personal 'inner light'? That our interactions with others and with the earth and its creatures is not what it could and should be?

Should a 'miracle' of 'enlightenment' transpire, it just may precipitate a return to the sanity of 'spirit'-focused humanity, with attendant egalitarian, truly democratic systems of political, economic and social organisation. It would, of course, be far simpler, faster, less destructive and painful if we were to approach transformation from the correct direction, vis-a-vis the point of realising the truth about us as equally-valuable, equally-worthy, equally-ordinary, humble, mutually-submitted spiritual sisters and brothers. Such is the only consciousness able to deliver lives of harmony, justice and peace.

It isn't reasonable – it isn't possible – to think effectively about any single aspect of this world in isolation from every other aspect. Wisdom traditions throughout all of history have grappled with the mystery of life, seeking what is 'elusive' understanding. Sensible science, sociology, philosophy, religion meet at a place called 'Oneness'; everything belongs as a part of the *One*. A 'see-er' – a mystic of any tradition – might look at a sheet of paper and see a rain cloud, understanding that the cloud produced rain to grow the tree that provided the wood from which the paper was made. She may see a woodsman honing his axe in preparation for cutting the tree, his wife at the stove preparing food, his children watching their mother at work and listening to her stories of life. She may perceive warmth from the sun invisibly lifting into the air moisture from the ocean, and a breeze transporting that moist air to rising land where it falls as rain nourishing the tree.

All parts of the *One*. All aspects of the sheet of paper. Could this be called relinking the unity of what we, in our profane, reductionist view of life, have fragmented? And is not this *relinking* the linguistic origin of the term *religion* – 're-ligare'; '*to bind again*'; to bind again to the Truth about us as profound spiritual beings? To our great detriment and that of the whole earth, religion has achieved notoriety over centuries by being highjacked by men in one way or another and for one reason or another; reasons generally including greed for wealth, power and control. Nothing to do with mature humanity. Paradoxically, this greed rejects the very source of the true riches and power being sought; the *inner light of Love* spoken of by the truly wise and *actually religious*.

In the last couple of hundred years in particular, in Australia and many other parts of the world, Christianity has been corrupted by association with the culture of capitalism. Capitalism results in rising prosperity for some. Prosperity is comfortable, pleasurable and seductive. Christians are not immune to the temptations of comfort and pleasure that come with prosperity. Being profane as well as religious – driven by ego as well as by spirit – Christians can and do succumb to the 'ego-defence' of 'justification'. The prosperity gospel of 'health and wealth' is a classic example: '*If you are rich, God is blessing you*'! "*God wants all his children to be wealthy and well*'. "*If you're sick or poor, you're somehow out of favour with God*", etc. Jesus didn't teach that! He told us to be impartial, to welcome the stranger, heal the sick, visit those in prison, feed the hungry, look after the widow, care for the earth, hold lightly to material things, share freely and generously. So does

Buddhism; compassion, kindness. So does moderate Islam; belief in the holy books, prayer, alms, fasting, pilgrimage.

Here in Australia, our 'Christian' forebears – the 'new-comers' to this well-inhabited land – did the most 'un-Christian' thing: they claimed the land as their own even though it was obvious that others were already here! Ego rationalisation comes easy to us humans, though, and, to our enduring shame and disgrace, we deemed the indigenous peoples as somehow 'less than human' and, therefore, it was OK to violate them, murder them and steal their land! Those crimes against humanity have still to be redressed. Sovereignty of this land has not been ceded. We new-comers are still illegal occupants and need to somehow put that injustice right. A good *start* would be to accept that fact, and acknowledge the 'Statement from the Heart'; honour the First Nations Peoples with an appropriate 'Voice' in parliament. And go on from there to do whatever is necessary to become a single, honouring and, thus, 'honourable' nation.

But how? How do we get from our present fragmentedness and division to a place of true community? Perhaps we could take a lesson from the 1996 Truth and Reconciliation Commission that followed the dismantling of Apartheid in South Africa. The wisdom of Nelson Mandela, Desmond Tutu and others convinced Government authorities that victims of the racial domination must be given a voice, and that voice honoured if the country was to be healed. Humility was required; humility to listen, deeply-hear, acknowledge and restore. Humility is a Divine quality; a quality arising from our deepest selves and a manifestation of true religion.

Who Needs Religion?

The evidence of our broken selves and world is that we all do! But to specify religion as church, mosque, synagogue, temple, ashram or some other grouped interest and set of prescriptions, is to miss it completely. Sectarian religions throughout the history of humankind separate, judge, vilify, impoverish, kill and destroy. Nothing *religious* in any of that. We have a challenge. Our challenge is to *relink* to the mystery often referred to in spiritual literature as our deepest self; the location of functional humanity animated by *inner light*; true religion that doesn't manifest the unjust means of capitalism or privileged white Christianity.

I wonder will we Australians '*make Australia fair*'. I do hope so. *Hope* is one of the ever-lasting 'big three', the other two 'companions' being '*Faith* and *Love*'. With faith – with belief in the Truth about us as bearers of a mysterious yet absolutely *real* Divine Image; with that consciousness it is possible that we will see clearly, survive and thrive. That miracle would require each of us to realise and submit to the *inner light of Love* – the only source of truth and justice and the common good; the good for *all* life on earth. We've already got what it takes. We've had it from birth. The only question is will we choose to remain in the ego's dualistic illusion of self-importance, need for control, imagined security, and comfort, or will we choose to *wake up*, access the humility and wisdom of our Love Nature, and exercise the courage and commitment to follow it to the *fairness*, desperately needed?

www.ingramcontent.com/pod-product-compliance
Lightning Source LLC
Chambersburg PA
CBHW011829020426
42334CB00027B/2993